THOMAS COOK
Travellers

ORLANDO

BY
ROGER ST PIERRE

Produced by AA Publishing

Written by Roger St Pierre,
with additional material by Paul Murphy

Original photography by Antony Souter

Edited, designed and produced by AA Publishing.
© The Automobile Association 1995.
Maps © The Automobile Association 1995.

Distributed in the United Kingdom by AA Publishing,
Norfolk House, Priestley Road, Basingstoke, Hampshire
RG24 9NY.

A CIP catalogue record for this book is available from the
British Library.

ISBN 0 7495 1011 0

The contents of this publication are believed correct at the time of
printing. Nevertheless, the publishers cannot accept responsibility for
any errors or omissions, or for changes in the details given in this guide,
or for the consequences of any reliance on the information provided by
the same. Assessments of attractions, hotels, restaurants and so forth are
based upon the author's own experience, and therefore descriptions
given in this guide necessarily contain an element of subjective opinion
which may not reflect the publisher's opinion or dictate a reader's own
experiences on another occasion.
**We have tried to ensure accuracy in this guide, but things do
change and we would be grateful if readers would advise us of
any inaccuracies they may encounter.**

Published by AA Publishing (a trading name of Automobile Association
Developments Limited, whose registered office is Norfolk House,
Priestley Road, Basingstoke, Hampshire RG24 9NY. Registered number
1878835) and the Thomas Cook Group Ltd.

Colour separation: BTB Colour Reproduction, Whitchurch,
Hampshire.

Printed by Edicoes ASA, Oporto, Portugal.

Cover picture: *Spaceship Earth, Epcot Center*
Title page: *fresh Florida oranges*
Above: *beer with a bite*

Contents

About this Book

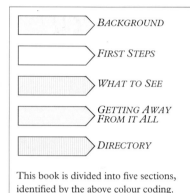

> BACKGROUND

> FIRST STEPS

> WHAT TO SEE

> GETTING AWAY FROM IT ALL

> DIRECTORY

This book is divided into five sections, identified by the above colour coding.

We've got a ticket to ride – how many can you collect during your visit?

Background gives an introduction to Orlando and its environs – its history, geography, politics, culture.

First Steps provides practical advice on arriving and getting around.

What to See is an alphabetical listing of places to visit, interspersed with walks and tours.

Getting Away From it All highlights places off the beaten track where it's possible to enjoy peace and quiet.

Finally, the **Directory** provides practical information – from shopping and entertainment to children and sport, including a section on business matters. Special highly illustrated features on specific aspects of Orlando appear throughout the book.

BACKGROUND

'The very name Florida
carried the message
of warmth and ease and
comfort. It was irresistible.'
JOHN STEINBECK
Travels with Charley, 1962

Introduction

*O*nce upon a time (and not so very long ago) there was a sleepy little town called Orlando. It lay in the middle of a mosquito-bitten, waterlogged scrub plain, miles from the ocean. A less likely setting for a holiday destination was hardly imaginable – until along came a man with a vision.

Orlando – 'the City Beautiful'

Walt Disney had already revolutionised the leisure industry with his original Disneyland in Los Angeles and he was now looking for a new site. His ambition was to build the biggest and best tourism attraction in the world. What he needed most was space – something Florida offered in abundance.

Today, four out of the world's top five paid-visitor attractions are located in Orlando (the exception, almost inevitably, is the original Disneyland). There's never a problem filling a fortnight in Orlando. The only difficulty is in deciding what not to see. A family could easily spend a week at Walt Disney World alone. But then there's Universal Studios, Sea World, Wet 'n' Wild, Splendid China, Church Street Station and, just a short drive away, other world-class attractions, such as Busch Gardens, the Kennedy Space Center, Cypress Gardens, Silver Springs and much more.

Even holidaymakers with no great interest in theme parks can find plenty to enjoy in and around Orlando – international-class galleries and museums, a multitude of shops, the most cosmopolitan restaurants, terrific sports facilities and, just out of town, a whole host of unspoilt natural attractions.

FLORIDA LOCATOR

FLORIDA

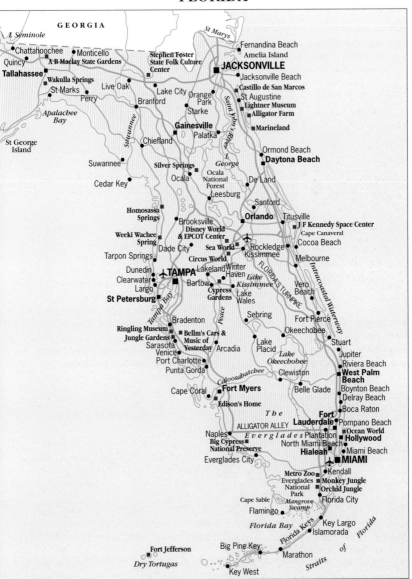

History

Some 8,000 to 10,000 years ago, long before any European saw Florida, Indians had settled here, and when the first Spaniards arrived in the 16th century, they found Apalachee and Timucuan Indians living in communities, with strong religious, family and social structures.

American Indians, Florida

1513

The Spanish explorer, Juan Ponce de León, lands near present-day St Augustine – possibly in search of the legendary Fountain of Youth, probably in search of gold. He names the land La Florida, after the date of his arrival, La Pascua Florida (the Spanish 'Eastertide of Flowers').

1528–39

Two more major Spanish expeditions, led by Pánfilo de Narváez and Hernando de Soto, arrive in the north of Florida in search of gold. Disease and Indians put paid to their hopes and no traces of settlement are left behind.

1564

French (Protestant) Huguenots found the settlement of Fort Caroline on the St John's river. The enraged (Catholic) Spain sends a force led by Pedro Menéndez de Avilés to remove the French. He does so with great loss of life and also founds St Augustine for Spain.

1702–4

After a 52-day siege the British capture St Augustine, though the Castillo remains intact.

1763–83

Florida comes under British control, but 20 years later it reverts to Spain.

1817–18

War breaks out between the Seminoles (Creek Indians from the Southern States who migrated to Florida) and the US Army.

1842

The tiny community of Jernigan (named after the Georgian settler Aaron Jernigan) is established around a wooden

The arrival of Spanish explorer Juan Ponce de Léon in 1513

fort used during the Seminole Wars, upon the site of present-day Orlando.

1845
Mosquito County, of which Jernigan is the main settlement, changes its name to Orange County, after its principal crop. Florida's population at this time is 66,500.

1850
Local trade has developed sufficiently in Jernigan to warrant the opening of a branch of the US Post Office.

1857
Jernigan changes its name to Orlando. Legend has it that this was in tribute to a US soldier, named Orlando Reeves, who heroically saved his company by sounding the alarm to warn of an Indian attack. He was killed in the attack.

late 1800s
Orlando attracts wealthy new citizens – successful business people from the North seeking a winter home with a more amenable climate. By now Orlando is known as 'the City Beautiful' and in 1885 Rollins College becomes the first private higher education school in Florida. Winter Park is developed around it over the next two decades.

1924–9
A land boom hits Florida with speculation reaching frantic levels in the southeast.

1961
The first American astronaut, Alan Shepherd, takes off from Cape Canaveral on Florida's northeast 'Space Coast'.

1965
Walt Disney buys up 28,000 acres

THOMAS COOK'S ORLANDO

Thomas Cook began tours to the USA almost immediately after the end of the Civil War. By the end of the 1880s the company had an American headquarters in New York which ran tours to Florida for the benefit of both British visitors and Americans anxious to escape the northern winter. Cook's Excursionist *of January 1889 devotes a full page to the choice of tours around Florida 'by rail and steamer', based on Jacksonville, which was convenient for arrivals from New York by sea and where the company had an office. A two-day circular tour via Orlando in those days cost $15.35, inclusive of meals and overnight accommodation.*

of land near Orlando for his new theme park project.

1971
Walt Disney World opens, originally just as the Magic Kingdom.

1982
Epcot opens.

1989
Disney–MGM Studios opens. The three Walt Disney World theme parks comprise the world's number one tourist destination and by the late 1980s are selling 30 million entrance tickets a year.

Indian totem pole

Geography

*O*rlando lies on the same latitude as the Canary Islands (just off the coast of Africa), and on the same longitude as London and Ontario. It is situated in the heart of central Florida with the Atlantic Ocean 47 miles to the east and the balmy Gulf of Mexico 100 miles to the west. This semi-tropical location holds many advantages for visitors, most notably, a hot sunny climate and a profusion of colourful flowers and exotic wildlife.

Terrain

Orlando stands just 75 feet above sea level, in the middle of a huge, flat plain, which gives way to low, gently rolling hills to the north. Distances in Florida are considerable. The peninsula is roughly equal in size to England and driving from Miami to Tallahassee is akin to travelling from Paris to Berlin or London to Frankfurt. However, despite low highway-speed limits, the flat terrain, the abundance of multi-lane freeways and the ease of parking on arrival all make relatively light of long journeys.

Flora and fauna

Surrounded by lakes, creeks and old logging canals, Orlando claims more acres of water than does Venice (near by, Ocala National Forest alone boasts nearly 1,000 named lakes). This, along with a gentle climate and acre-upon-acre of woodlands and protected forests, provides for an abundance of wildlife. Many unusual and endangered species are to be seen here, including Florida's famous alligators (see page 130) and manatees (sea-cows – see pages 92–3).

The heavily developed business district of central Orlando offers not only carefully manicured lawns and flower beds but also several fine parks and many well-tended lakes, while a more natural, wilderness-style environment can be found a very short drive away. Even within city limits however, it is possible to see alligators, turtles and snakes sunning themselves on the water banks. Indeed, locals are not overly shocked if they find such creatures on their lawns! Otters are common too, while birdlife ranges from the commonplace vultures, egrets and mockingbirds to much rarer species (see pages 128–9).

Strange unworldly-looking mangroves grow to the south of Orlando

A relaxing way to explore Fort Lauderdale

The climate to the north of Florida breeds a temperate flora but as you head further south it favours lush, semi-tropical vegetation. Pines flourish in the Ocala National Forest, just north of Orlando while to the south of town, around Lake Okeechobee, are prairie grasslands. In between these areas are springs and swamps but the most popular sub-tropical images of swaying palm trees and wild extensive swamp-lands are to be found only much further south. Spanish moss (a grey beard-like bromeliad) can be seen, draped picturesquely from many an urban tree.

Man has made his mark on the natural environment, too. Centred around the Clermont area, a staggering 17 million orange trees cover some 2,000 square miles (see pages 166–7). Yet wherever you drive around Orlando, you will see the sad, withered skeletons of

orange trees killed in the last big freeze. Some farmers have doggedly replanted; others have turned to less sensitive plants like strawberries and sweetcorn, or to tourism.

Climate
Fortunately Orlando is spared the worst effects of the fearsome hurricanes which can devastate Florida's exposed coasts between June and November, and would have a near perfect climate for a holiday resort were it not for the generally high levels of humidity, which become decidedly uncomfortable in summer. Fortunately cars and buildings are universally equipped with efficient air-conditioning systems to make light of this problem. (Don't forget – for them to work properly – it is essential to keep windows and patio doors properly closed). Heating is only needed on rare chilly winter nights.

CENTRAL FLORIDA

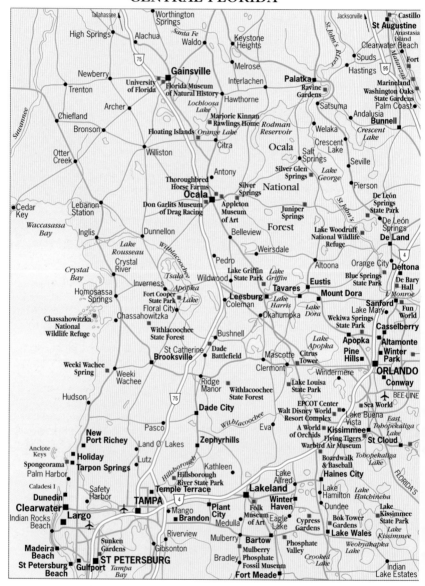

Tallahassee · Worthington Springs · Jacksonville · Castillo · St Augustine · Anastasia Island · Clearwater Beach

High Springs · Alachua · Santa Fe · Keystone Heights · Spuds · Fort

Waldo · Melrose · Hastings · 95

Newberry · University of Florida · Florida Museum of Natural History · Interlachen · Palatka · Ravine Gardens · Marineland · Washington Oaks State Gardens · Palm Coast

Trenton · Lochloosa Lake · Hawthorne · Satsuma · Andalusia

Chiefland · Archer · Marjorie Kinnan Rawlings Home · Rodman Reservoir · Welaka · Bunnell · Crescent Lake

Bronson · Floating Islands · Orange Lake · Citra · Ocala · Salt Springs · Crescent Lake · Seville

Otter Creek · Williston · Antony · Silver Glen Springs · Lake George · Pierson

Cedar Key · Lebanon Station · Thoroughbred Horse Farms · Ocala · Silver Springs · National · De León Springs State Park

Waccasassa Bay · Don Garlits Museum of Drag Racing · Appleton Museum of Art · Juniper Springs · De León Springs

Inglis · Dunnellon · Belleview · Forest · Lake Woodruff National Wildlife Refuge · De Land

Lake Rousseau · Weirsdale

Crystal Bay · Crystal River · Withlacoochee · Pedro · Lake Griffin State Park · Lake Griffin · Altoona · Orange City · Deltona

Inverness · Tsala · Wildwood · Eustis · Blue Springs State Park · De Bary Hall · L'Monroe

Homosassa Springs · Fort Cooper State Park · Apopka Lake · Leesburg · Lake Harris · Tavares · Mount Dora · Sanford · Fun World

Chassahowitzka National Wildlife Refuge · Floral City · Chassahowitzka · Coleman · Okahumpka · Lake Dora · Wekiwa Springs State Park · Lake Mary · Casselberry

Withlacoochee State Forest · Bushnell · Lake Apopka · Apopka · Altamonte

Weeki Wachee Spring · Weeki Wachee · St Catherine · Dade Battlefield · Brooksville · Mascotte · Citrus Tower · Pine Hills · Winter Park · ORLANDO

Clermont · Windermere · Conway

Hudson · Ridge Manor · Withlacoochee State Forest · Lake Louisa State Park · BEE-LINE

EPCOT Center · Sea World

Dade City · Walt Disney World Resort Complex · Lake Buena Vista · East Tohopekaliga Lake

New Port Richey · Pasco · Eva · A World of Orchids · Kissimmee · Flying Tigers · St Cloud

Anclote Keys · Land O' Lakes · Zephyrhills · Warbird Air Museum

Spongeorama · Holiday · Lutz · Boardwalk & Baseball · Tohopekaliga Lake

Palm Harbor · Tarpon Springs · Kathleen · Haines City

Caladesi I · Safety Harbor · Hillsborough River State Park · Lake Alfred · Lake Hamilton · Lake Hatchineha

Dunedin · Temple Terrace · Lakeland · Dundee · Lake Kissimmee

Clearwater · TAMPA · Winter Haven · Bok Tower Gardens · Lake Kissimmee State Park

Indian Rocks Beach · Largo · Mango · Plant City · Folk Museum of Art · Eagle Lake · Cypress Gardens · Lake Wales · Lake Kissimmee

Brandon · Medulla

Madeira Beach · Sunken Gardens · Riverview · Mulberry · Bartow · Phosphate Valley · Weohyakapka Lake

St Petersburg · Gibsonton · Mulberry · Crooked Lake · Indian Lake Estates

St Petersburg Beach · Gulfport · Tampa Bay · Bradley · Phosphate Fossil Museum · Fort Meade

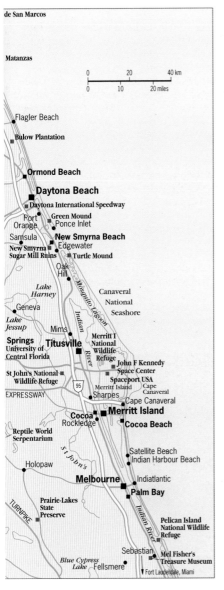

de San Marcos

Matanzas

0   20   40 km
0   10   20 miles

Flagler Beach

Bulow Plantation

Ormond Beach

Daytona Beach

Daytona International Speedway

Port   Green Mound
Orange   Ponce Inlet

Samsula   **New Smyrna Beach**
New Smyrna   Edgewater
Sugar Mill Ruins   Turtle Mound

Oak
Hill

Lake
Harney   Canaveral
National
Geneva   Seashore
Lake
Jessup   Mims

Springs   **Titusville**   Merritt I
University of   National
Central Florida   Wildlife
Refuge

St John's National   John F Kennedy
Wildlife Refuge   Space Center
95   Spaceport USA
EXPRESSWAY   Merritt Island   Cape
Sharpes   Canaveral

Cocoa   **Merritt Island**
Rockledge   **Cocoa Beach**
Reptile World
Serpentarium

Satellite Beach
Indian Harbour Beach
Holopaw

Melbourne   Indiatlantic
Palm Bay

Prairie-Lakes
State
Preserve

Pelican Island
National Wildlife
Refuge

Sebastian   Mel Fisher's
Blue Cypress   Treasure Museum
Lake   Fellsmere   Fort Lauderdale, Miami

A suntan is almost an inevitable souvenir of a holiday in Orlando, for abundant sunshine is the year-round norm, even in mid-winter, when daily highs often reach 72°F (22°C). However, the thermometer sometimes plummets right down to freezing point on winter nights, so it is worth taking some warm clothing. Temperatures in the 90°F (33°C) range are common in summer, when afternoon thunder showers are quite common. Do be careful of the sun. Even on cloudy days, it is more powerful than you might realise and many people end up burned because of their failure to take appropriate precautions. Restraint, and a good sunscreen are called for throughout the year.

The people and the economy
Orlando is still rapidly expanding, with immigration currently running at around 1,000 new residents a week (of course, not all stay!). The area's permanent population is about one million but is swollen each year by around 14 times that number of tourists.

The area's dependence on tourism is reflected in the fact that visitor-related activities account for one-in-four of all jobs, representing an industry worth more than $5 billion annually. Walt Disney World alone employs some 35,000 permanent staff and is the biggest employer in Central Florida. However, Central Florida, and Metro Orlando in particular, is becoming an increasingly important business centre where a number of large American and international corporations have established major offices and manufacturing plants. One important attraction is the ease of communication offered by Orlando's geographic location at the crossroads of Florida.

Culture

*B*rash, bright, fun, and bang-up-to-date – that's the popular image of Orlando. But there's a more deeply rooted and altogether more cultured side to things as well. Yes, this is essentially a young community, but it grew from roots which run deep. What's more, while the theme parks and other key attractions are aimed squarely at a family audience, the city also has appeal for an older, more refined generation. These are the very kind of people who first put it on the map in the early years of this century when it became a favoured location for second homes and an attractive place to retire. Museums, art galleries, ballet and opera are all part of the city's appeal.

In this middle-class haven, the per capita income is way above the national average. Nearly 700,000 people, with an average age of 32, are employed in the area and thousands more move in each year. It is claimed that more than 30,000 new jobs have been created here over the past five years. Given the pleasant environment and such an abundance of employment opportunities, the work

Left: taking time out
Below: the fine Orlando Museum of Art at Loch Haven

With such a lot to see and do – let Thomas Cook help out

ethic is good and Orlando has managed to avoid the deprivation, social disorder and urban decay problems which have blighted other cities. And despite being tainted with the adverse publicity generated by violent crime in other parts of Florida, Orlando has a crime rate which is far lower than that of most cities in Europe or in North America.

Having a nice day

'Have a nice day' has long slipped into common usage and is often a bland throw-away remark. Yet despite all the obviously false attempts at sincerity and the ridiculously unnecessary introductions that every member of serving staff feels compelled to offer you, service in Florida often comes with a genuine smile. Give the staff the benefit of the doubt, suspend your cynicism and be prepared to talk to people who are interested in 'the old country', or about what it's like in Europe.

Thomas Cook's Tip

In keeping with its long tradition of looking after the traveller, Thomas Cook offers visitors to Orlando a unique 'one-stop' shopping facility through its Guest Services desks, located in hotel lobbies across the area. Everything from foreign currency exchange and the cashing of travellers' cheques to ticket purchase for major theme parks, car hire and cruise bookings, dinner, golf and tennis reservations, and even babysitting services, can be easily and quickly arranged by experienced and trained staff.

By providing for theme park admission through a personalised voucher system, Thomas Cook affords added security for its clients. If a voucher should be lost or stolen, it can be cancelled and promptly replaced at no additional charge.

For further information while in Orlando, contact: Thomas Cook Guest Services (tel: (407) 352 1171).

Politics

On the surface, politics do not seem to play much of a part in the well-ordered life of Orlando. Quite simply, the town goes about its business, and that business is tourism. However, the rapid expansion of the city over the past three decades is beginning to cause concern and the city authorities, the local business community and local residents alike are now aware of the serious need to address environmental issues, especially since much of the pressure for change is coming from ecologically aware tourists, the very people who put money into Orlando's communal pocket.

Besides destroying the environment of some of the earth's rarest wild creatures, ad hoc development has produced many eyesores and while some remarkably good and inventive architecture is to be admired, too much of it has been bland or tacky and built to a price. Zoning regulations are now becoming stiffer and more work is being done to preserve the remaining habitat. Thankfully it is now widely recognised that Florida's wildlife, especially the profusion of birds, is an important tourist attraction in itself.

Disastrous alterations to the water table – damming, drainage and diverting watercourses in the name of both agriculture and building development, are now being redressed. Crime and the personal safety of visitors and residents alike constitutes another political hot potato, though the truth is that Orlando has an enviably low incidence of robberies and assaults compared to most other cities in North America and Europe.

Orlando's politicians, of both parties, now recognise that the good health of the local tourism industry is of vital importance. They see their involvement in responsibly conceived programmes to improve the visitor experience as a sure vote catcher from local citizens who have come to enjoy, and rely upon, the tourist dollar.

Orlando's impressive
City Hall

FIRST STEPS

'Orlando is like an enormous
plateful of the most calorific,
imaginative, appetising
junk food you will ever taste.'
LINDSAY HUNT,
AA *Essential Orlando and Walt Disney World*

First Steps

*I*t is a mistake to think of Orlando as a city in the conventional sense – with most of the attractions concentrated into a central area which can be covered on foot or by public transport. Though it has a lively downtown business and night-life area, Orlando is essentially an urban sprawl.

Before doing anything else, it is worth paying a visit to the Orlando Visitor Information Center, Mercado Mediterranean Village, International Drive for useful brochures and up-to-date information on where to go and what to see (open: daily 8am–8pm; tel: (407) 363–5876). While you are here look out for discount coupons on leaflets, in tourist information magazines, in newspapers and the like. These can save you several dollars on eating out, admission fees, shopping and even accommodation. Most car rental desks also carry a wide range of leaflets covering the various attractions, and provide free road maps too.

Parking is never a problem

When to go

School holidays bring European visitors and Americans flocking into Orlando. Package tours at such times are more expensive and the combination of oppressive heat and valuable time spent waiting for rides, restaurant seats and the like, can mar a visit.

If sunbathing and outdoor swimming are not your top priority, in-between months like November and February have their attraction. Orlando is very much a year-round resort.

GETTING THERE
Air

Besides its links with the rest of the world, Orlando International Airport is served by an extensive network of domestic services, with cheap off-peak fares making excursions to other parts of the States thoroughly practical.

Train and bus

Amtrak trains rattle right through the centre of Orlando on their way from New York to Miami, while long-haul Greyhound bus services are the cheapest way of reaching further-flung destinations. Orlando itself has sparse public transport provision.

GETTING AROUND
Travelling by car

Distances are considerable so don't be misled by tourist maps. The drive between downtown Orlando and Walt

Disney World, for example, takes at least 30 minutes even on the I-4 highway. However, as you will soon learn, this is very much the land of the automobile and a good network of wide, well-surfaced roads ensures quick and easy access to most places. Car hire (car rental) and petrol (gasoline) are both inexpensive by European standards. Filling stations are invariably self-serve, and open 24 hours. They are clean, convenient and usually offer more than just fuel.

In this car-borne society, parking provision is a major priority and ample space is available almost everywhere. However, meters operate downtown and you should be aware of tow-away zones.

Taxis are relatively cheap per mile for those who do not wish to drive, but the miles soon clock up.

Like most American cities, Orlando's streets follow a grid system and street-name signs indicate both the house

A taxi from the airport is just a few dollars

numbering and the north/south/east/west directions. Route signs on major highways are generally mounted on overhead gantries, but unfortunately these only offer minimal information (sometimes just the route number or a single destination), so it's important to study maps before you set off. The number indicated on other roadside signs (without any direction arrow), is not the road you are on but the number of the next turn-off.

Another unfamiliar convention is that traffic lights are mounted across junctions, rather than in front of them and, traffic is allowed to turn right against the red light (provided that the road is clear). Give yourself a day or two to acclimatise, however, and you will discover that driving here is far less hectic than in Europe.

Planning your time

Getting the best from your visit demands forward planning so that not too much time is spent pounding the highway network. It is the nature of an Orlando holiday that, just as a lot of time will be spent travelling from place to place, so it is also essential not to try to pack too much into one day. Long theme park queues at busy periods, with waiting

ORLANDO

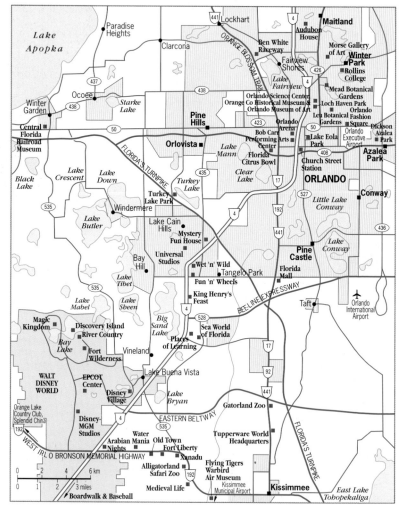

Waiting for the bus in Orlando

times of more than an hour for the most popular rides, and the sheer size and complexity of most of the attractions, will leave you feeling cheated if time constraints mean cutting a visit short. You'll need a full day in all the major theme parks, and that means an early start. Make dining reservations on arrival, and save shopping until the end of the visit. Tackle the major rides early in the morning or late in the afternoon, when queues are at their smallest.

Currency

Plastic talks in America and credit cards are essential for car rental, hotel bills and the like. In out-of-town areas (and sometimes even in town), visitors will find problems getting banks to change foreign currency. The good news, however, is that US-dollar travellers'

cheques are accepted as cash almost everywhere with change given in dollars and at no exchange penalty. Be aware that bank notes are all the same colour. Check their denominations carefully before you hand them over.

Lifestyle

In a region dedicated to good times and blessed with long hours of sunshine, the outdoor life has considerable attractions. Easy-going and hospitable, but never

> Beware, American water is always heavily chlorinated and a dip in the hotel or villa swimming pool can result in stinging eyes. If you want to swim, as opposed to just splash about, it's worth bringing a pair of goggles.

Cool and casual is the order of the day

slow to take up a business opportunity, the locals have made ample provision for all leisure tastes. You can rent bicycles and fishing gear, or even a luxury houseboat for a week or two. Barbecues are a way of life, but pavement society does not really exist on the same scale as in Europe; most Americans prefer air-conditioned comfort inside a restaurant. Be prepared to chat; waiters and waitresses are often friendly and American holidaymakers are particularly eager to talk to Europeans.

Language
Given that a third of all overseas visitors come from the UK and that British programmes like *EastEnders* and *Emmerdale Farm* are popular features on public service TV, Orlando natives have few problems coping with British accents and dialect. Also, because of the sheer number of immigrants, most other European visitors will not have to go far before meeting someone who speaks their own language. Spanish is very widely spoken, thanks to the large numbers of Latin American immigrants working in the hotel and catering industries, while many Americans study French or German at school or have recent European origins.

But Winston Churchill was right when he said 'The British and Americans are two nations divided by a common language' for many words have embarrassingly different meanings. The British might walk on their 'pavement' – the Americans drive on theirs!

Dress
Because of its status as a holiday resort, Orlando has a very relaxed dress code, with casual trousers, sports jackets and open-necked shirts being acceptable in the most formal of restaurants. However, the penchant for running air-conditioning at full belt might leave women wishing they had brought a shoulder wrap. Coming into the lobby from the pool still wearing bathing gear is bad form but nobody will take notice if you are in tennis kit.

A lightweight raincoat is useful in summer, as showers, though short, can be torrential, while winter visitors should bring a sweater and a heavier jacket or top coat.

Tipping
Tipping is an essential part of the Florida service ethic and often wrongfoots European visitors. From the bell boy who takes your suitcase to the waiter who takes your order, a tip is always expected even if it is not earned. If you don't agree with tipping be prepared to defend your corner! (See **Tipping**, page 189.)

WHAT TO SEE

'Central Florida – a study
in reality suspension,
brought to your
imagination by the
nation's finest fantasy
makers.'
FLORIDA TOURIST BOARD

Orlando

*T*here is far more to Orlando than just theme parks. If you want to get away from all those artifical 'worlds' and 'lands' and see something of the ordinary everyday culture of Orlando, take a look at some of the following pleasantly low-key visitor attractions. All are within easy reach of town and are light on the pocket.

[Note: all location references are measured from Church Street Station at the centre of downtown Orlando.]

CHURCH STREET STATION
Downtown Orlando's premier evening entertainment spot (see pages 144–5).

FLORIDA CITRUS BOWL
This massive 72,000-seater stadium just west of downtown was recently face-lifted for its role as a soccer World Cup host venue. Besides the annual Citrus Bowl American football tournament each January – the Bowl stages National Football League pre-season matches and Division One college football games. Monster truck racing, supercross races, mud racing, concerts and other special events are also held here.

Location: 2 miles west of downtown. 1610 West Church Street, Orlando. Tel: (407) 849–2000.

LOCH HAVEN PARK
A pleasant retreat catering more for local residents than thrill-seeking tourists. As well as being a venue for kite flyers, picnickers, strolling couples and families, the park offers three interesting museums – Orange County Historical Museum (see below), Orlando Museum of Art and Orlando Science Center and John Young Planetarium (see opposite) plus Fire Station No 3, with its displays of fire-fighting history.
Location: 4 miles northeast of downtown. Take Exit 43 (Princeton Street) off I–4, then drive a mile east. Tel: (407) 898–8320. Open: Tuesday to Friday 10am–4pm, Saturday and Sunday 1–5pm. Admission charge.

ORANGE COUNTY HISTORICAL MUSEUM
Indian relics provide a starting point for a collection which traces the development of Mosquito County into today's Greater Orlando. The artefacts of the 'crackers' – cattle men renowned for their skill with a rawhide whip – are particularly interesting.
Location: 4 miles northeast of downtown. 812 East Rollins Street, Loch Haven Park.

Above and opposite: Orlando Museum of Art, Loch Haven

Tel: (407) 897–6350. Open: Monday to Saturday 9am–5pm, Sunday noon–5pm. Admission charge.

ORLANDO ARENA

This multi-purpose arena in the downtown Orlando Centroplex holds up to 15,000 spectators. It is home to the Orlando Predators in the Arena Football League, and the city's National Basketball Association franchise side, Orlando Magic (starring superstar Shaquille O'Neal). Concerts, ice spectaculars, rodeos and other events are also staged here.
Location: 1 mile west of downtown. Orlando Centroplex. Tel: (407) 849–2020.

ORLANDO MUSEUM OF ART

The Pre-Columbian gallery of this fine museum contains some 250 rare pieces, dating from 1200BC to AD1500, which give a fascinating insight into American culture before the arrival of the Europeans. Special exhibitions are shown on a rotational basis, along with the museum's own extensive collection of African and 20th-century American art.
Location: 4 miles northeast of downtown. 2416 North Mills Avenue, Loch Haven, Orlando. Tel: (407) 896–4231. Open:

Tuesday to Saturday 9am–5pm, Sunday noon–5pm. Admission charge.

ORLANDO SCIENCE CENTER AND JOHN YOUNG PLANETARIUM

The hands-on exhibits in this small complex make it particularly appealing to inquisitive children. Natural history, physical science and health matters are all covered. The popular Planetarium presents daily starshows, exciting weekend laser shows and 'cosmic concerts'.
Location: 4 miles northeast of downtown. 810 East Rollins Street, Loch Haven, Orlando. Tel: (407) 896–7151. Open: Monday to Thursday and Saturday 9am–5pm, Friday 9am–9pm, Sunday noon–5pm. Admission charge.

TURKEY LAKE PARK

Turkey Lake Park is a popular local amenity offering beaches, a swimming pool, a 200-foot fishing pier, canoe rentals, hiking and cycling trails, a children's playground and a petting zoo.
Location: 8 miles southwest of downtown. 3401 Hiawassee Road, Orlando. Open: daily 9.30am–7pm. Admission charge.

A FLYING VISIT

Thousands of visitors are getting a new perspective of the Sunshine State by taking to the air. For most this means a hot-air balloon flight – suspended from a wicker gondola beneath a billowing cloud of brilliantly coloured fabric, floating on the gentle breeze.

There are numerous operators in the region who, for around $150, will take you up into the blue yonder and serve you a champagne breakfast. Try the Central Florida Balloon Co (tel: (407) 895–1686), Orange Blossom Balloons (tel: (407) 239–7677) or Rise and Float Balloon Tours (tel: (407) 352–8191). Or if you intend visiting Church Street Station during your stay (see pages 144–5) it's worth considering Rosie O'Grady's Balloon Flights, as the price includes admission to Church Street, and is valid for a whole year (tel: (407) 841–8787). Aerial

Adventures (tel: (407) 841–UPUP) offer both conventional balloon rides and blimp tours.

A noisier, but just as spectacular way of getting a bird's-eye view, is to take a helicopter tour. Six different options are available from the Falcon Helicopter Service (tel: (407) 352–1753). If you really believe 'things just ain't what they used to be' and you fancy a trip to the Florida Keys (or other

A ride in a helicopter is very reasonably priced

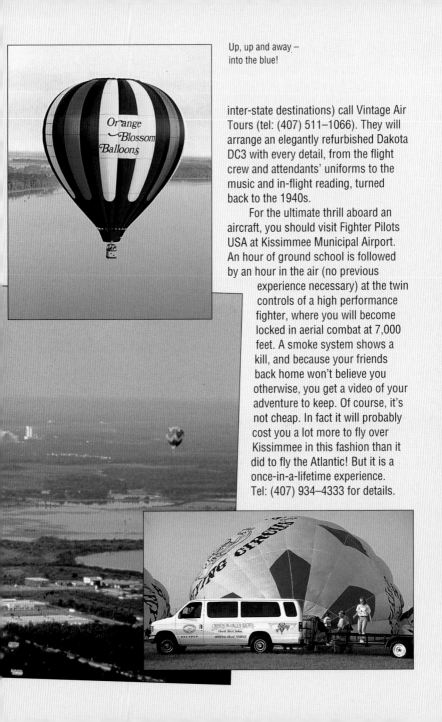

Up, up and away –
into the blue!

inter-state destinations) call Vintage Air Tours (tel: (407) 511–1066). They will arrange an elegantly refurbished Dakota DC3 with every detail, from the flight crew and attendants' uniforms to the music and in-flight reading, turned back to the 1940s.

For the ultimate thrill aboard an aircraft, you should visit Fighter Pilots USA at Kissimmee Municipal Airport. An hour of ground school is followed by an hour in the air (no previous experience necessary) at the twin controls of a high performance fighter, where you will become locked in aerial combat at 7,000 feet. A smoke system shows a kill, and because your friends back home won't believe you otherwise, you get a video of your adventure to keep. Of course, it's not cheap. In fact it will probably cost you a lot more to fly over Kissimmee in this fashion than it did to fly the Atlantic! But it is a once-in-a-lifetime experience. Tel: (407) 934–4333 for details.

International Drive

*I*nternational Drive is the brash, bustling, neon-lit High Street of Orlando, its sidewalks fronted with a vast array of shops, eating places and tourist attractions. It is also the artery which feeds visitors into the major theme parks, from Universal Studios past Wet 'n' Wild and right on down to Walt Disney World.

FUN 'N' WHEELS

Here are go-carts, bumper cars and bumper boats to suit all ages and even miniaturised two-seater tanks, which fight it out on a replicated battlefield. A Ferris wheel, mini-golf, a skid pan, a video arcade and a waterslide add to the fun. *Location: on Sand Lake Road (SR 482), one block east of International Drive junction. Tel: (407) 351–5651. Open: daily (summer) 10am–midnight; Monday to Friday 4–11pm, 10am–midnight, weekends (winter). Admission charge.*

Mystery Fun House – located just across from Universal Studios

MEL FISHER'S WORLD OF TREASURE

Explorer Mel Fisher has dedicated his life to recovering treasures from the Caribbean and the Atlantic. The most notable finds here come from a fleet of 12 Spanish and French galleons, lost during a fearsome storm in 1622 together with some 700 lives. The treasure trove includes gold ingots, doubloons, jewels, and many items of barnacle-encrusted ship's tackle. The story of the painstaking and sometimes dangerous work of treasure hunting is brought to life through a fascinating short film. *Location: just off the south end of International Drive, 8586 Palm Parkway. Tel: (407) 589–0435. Open: daily 10am–11pm. Admission charge.*

MYSTERY FUN HOUSE

A free bus service takes visitors the short distance from International Drive to Mystery Fun House, with its famous maze of distorting mirrors. A 'Forbidden Temple', based on an Indiana Jones adventure is just one of 15 'Chambers of Surprise' and there are dozens of laser and video games in what is Orlando's premier amusement arcade. There is also mini-golf and, for an additional charge, the all-action Starbase Omega laser game. *Location: 5767 Major Boulevard, off International Drive. Tel: (407) 351–3355. Open: daily 10am–10pm (later in peak season). Admission charge.*

INTERNATIONAL DRIVE

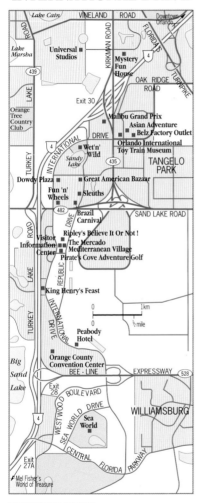

8601 International Drive. Tel: (407) 352–7378. Open: daily 9am–11.30pm. Admission charge.

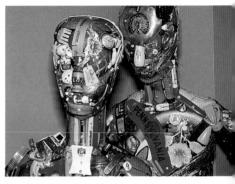

Recycled robots at Ripley's

RIPLEY'S BELIEVE IT OR NOT!
Based on Robert Ripley's eponymous world-circulated newspaper trivia column, this bizarre attraction chronicles the odd, the scarcely believable and the truly outlandish. Exhibits include freaks of nature (among them a genuine two-headed calf), oddities like Three-Ball Charlie – who could put three pool balls in his mouth and whistle at the same time – and fascinating illusions. There's a two-storey-high replica of the Eiffel Tower, a 1907 Rolls Royce made from more than a million matchsticks, a Mona Lisa made of toast and a portrait of Vincent Van Gogh created from 10,000 picture postcards. Finally, beware the instructions to have a go at 'girning' (face pulling), for it's a two-way mirror you are looking into and the people on the other side can see exactly what you are doing. Don't worry though, it will be your turn to laugh at someone else a few minutes later!
8201 International Drive, Orlando. Tel: (407) 363–4418. Open: daily 10am–11pm (later in peak season). Admission charge.

PIRATE'S COVE
This lavishly landscaped miniature-golf course follows a skull and crossbones theme. Players putt through mountain caves, over bridges and under waterfalls with two different 18-hole challenges.

Downtown Orlando

Downtown Orlando is a mix of towering sky-scrapers and elegant refurbished Victorian struc-tures. The city took its shape between the 1920s and the 1940s and exhibits many of the architec-tural fads which were fashionable during this period – from the Chicago Commercial look to Spanish red-tiles and, of course, art deco. The current movement is neo-Victorian which provides a strong contrast with the city's ultra-modern tower blocks. Church Street Station, ambitiously renovated in the last two decades to become the city's entertainment mecca (see pages 144–5), is a good starting point for this walk. *Allow around an hour.*

Start at the railway crossing on Church Street and walk east. Amtrak's Silver Meteor and Silver Star pass through here each day. Parked in a railroad siding is the vintage steam engine which featured in John Wayne's Wings Of Eagles.

1 OLD ORLANDO RAILROAD DEPOT

The influence of the Depot's Russian architect is evident by the onion dome atop this 1889 edifice. It is listed in the National Register of Historic Places. Now Amtrak has a new

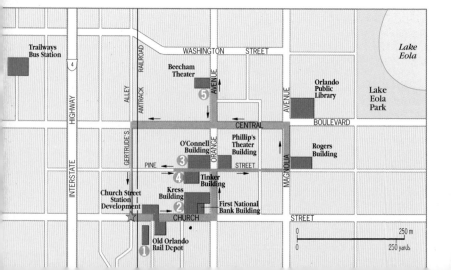

station down the line, the Depot has become a bustling mix of museum and shopping mall and a major magnet for tourists.
Stroll east along Church Street.

2 KRESS BUILDING
Built in 1936 this streamlined former 'nickel-and-dime' store is a classic of the art deco genre of architecture which took Florida by storm. Next door is the ornate Egyptian-styled First National Bank Building, constructed in 1929.
Turn left on to Orange Avenue, then left again and walk a few yards down Pine Street, Orlando's original main thoroughfare.

3 O'CONNELL BUILDING
This is one of the district's oldest buildings, opened in 1886, though its original spectacular exterior has now been sadly hidden by a somewhat bland façade. A cheery mural, painted on its Pine Street wall, depicts the street's colourful past.

4 TINKER BUILDING
Major league baseball player, Joe Tinker, turned to real estate and benefited from Florida's 1920s land boom to become a multi-millionaire. His building, once blighted with an aluminium-siding exterior, has been faithfully restored to its original glory and is now deservedly on the National Register of Historic Landmarks.
Retrace your steps and cross Orange Avenue, staying on Pine Street. Notice Phillip's Theater Building – Orlando's first cinema, later a store. Turn left on to Magnolia Avenue, glancing at the tin-clad Rogers Building, then left again on to Central Boulevard, before taking a right turn back on to Orange Avenue.

5 BEECHAM THEATER
This classic vaudeville showcase has had a rather chequered history. Despite recent attempts to revive its fortunes in various guises, this rather down-at-heel old lady sadly has still to find its niche in Orlando's current entertainment scene.
Retrace your steps to Central Boulevard, turn right, then left into Gertrude's Alley, which was Orlando's widest street until railway tracks were laid right down the middle of it.

Sun Bank Tower, Church Street Station

Kissimmee

*S*ome 20 miles south of downtown Orlando, the one-time 'hick town' of Kissimmee has capitalised on its proximity to Walt Disney World by becoming Central Florida's great vacation dormitory. Here you can find hotel accommodation at every level, from basic motels to exclusive luxury suites. Prestigious names like Marriott and Hyatt are represented alongside dubious establishments which rent rooms by the hour. But Kissimmee isn't just accommodation, it also has many worthy tourist attractions of its own.

Kissimmee's main street, US 192, is officially designated as the Irlo Bronson Memorial Highway. Locals call it the 'Tourist Trap Trail' after its profusion of night spots, fast-food restaurants, cheap motels, mini-golf courses, amusement arcades and go-kart tracks

The hub of this undignified sprawl is the Old Town complex, though confusingly this is not the oldest part of Kissimmee. That honour lies with Broadway Avenue.

Roadside attractions at Kissimmee

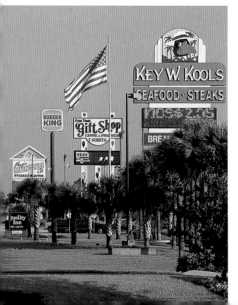

AIRBOAT RENTALS U–DRIVE

If you don't fancy the long drive south to ride an airboat through the Everglades, this is the next best thing. And here you can actually pilot your own craft through an unspoiled wilderness that seems a world away from the neon and plastic of US 192.
Location: 9 miles southeast of Old Town. 4266 W Vine Street, Kissimmee. Tel: (407) 847–3672. Open: daily 9am–5pm.

ALLIGATOR SAFARI ZOO

Not to be confused with Gatorland (also in Kissimmee, see opposite) this is a smaller establishment which features animals from around the world as well as the famous Florida reptiles.
Location: 4 miles east of Old Town. 4508 W Irlo Bronson Memorial Highway. Tel: (407) 396–1012. Open: daily 8.30am–dusk. Admission charge.

BROADWAY AVENUE

Kissimmee's historic old main street, Broadway Avenue, has retained its small-town flavour, with traditional country-store fronts; Makinson's hardware outlet – complete with its horse-shaped and bullet-riddled tin sign – is a notable example.

Just off Broadway on Monument Avenue, there's a bizarre monument to the US, made up from a pastiche of old

Feeding time is always frantic at Gatorland Zoo – 'Alligator Capital of the World'

memorabilia, topped by the fluttering Stars and Stripes.

South of Kissimmee lies the old Florida of wide-open spaces where cattle ranching is still a very important activity and cattle auctions are held at Broadway's Livestock Market every Wednesday morning.
Location: 8 miles southeast of Old Town. Broadway is the southern extension of US17–92/US441 (South Orange Blossom Trail).

FLYING TIGERS WARBIRD AIR MUSEUM

Based at the local airfield, this working museum preserves World War II airplanes from several nations in pristine flying condition. There are guided tours of the exhibits and workshops and flying demonstrations occasionally take place.
Location: 6 miles southeast of Old Town. 231 North Hoagland Boulevard, Kissimmee. Tel: (407) 933–1942. Open: Monday to Saturday 9am–5.30pm; Sunday 9am–5pm. Admission charge.

FORT LIBERTY

This is a spin-off from the popular Wild Bill's Wild West dinner show (see page 141) which is also held here. It purports to replicate a traditional Western fort and a Red Indian village, including a 'Trading Post' of 20 theme shops and the Brave Warrior Wax Museum.
5260 W Irlo Bronson Memorial Highway, Kissimmee. Tel: (407) 363–3510. Open: daily 10am–9pm. Admission charge to Wax Museum.

GATORLAND ZOO

This is claimed to be the world's largest alligator farm, with a collection of over 5,000 'gators. These primeval reptiles grow from new hatchlings to 17-feet long monsters. Walkways cross their cypress-swamp habitat and the narrow-gauge Gatorland Express winds through the property. Visitors can watch 'gator wrestling and there is a 10-acre breeding marsh to explore. An entertaining and educational show entitled Snakes Of Florida introduces the zoo's other prime inhabitants.

Under development are a Crocodiles Of The World exhibit and a Cracker Village, modelled after a local early 20th-century settlement.
Location: 16 miles northeast of Old Town. 14501 South Orange Blossom Trail (US441 South), Kissimmee, Orlando. Tel: (407) 855–5496. Open: daily 8am–dusk. Admission charge.

Green turtle

speciality shops and restaurants. Don't miss the beautifully crafted wonderful wooden trains of Walter T Potter in the Great Train Store and Exhibit (admission charge).
Location: 2 miles east of I–4 exit 25. 5770 Irlo Bronson Memorial Highway, Kissimmee. Tel: (407) 396–4888. Open: 10am–10pm. Free.

OSCEOLA COUNTY HISTORICAL MUSEUM & SPENCE-LANIER PIONEER CENTER

If you'd like to know what Kissimmee looked like around the turn of the century visit this beautiful nature preserve where you can see unspoiled countryside and rural life exhibits.
Location: 7 miles southeast of Old Town. 750 N Bass Road, Kissimmee. Tel: (407) 396–8644. Open: Monday to Saturday 10am–4pm, Sunday 1–4pm. Admission by donation.

REPTILE WORLD SERPENTARIUM

Should you be unlucky enough to be bitten by one of Florida's poisonous snakes, this is where the doctor will probably get his anti-venom serum from. Rattlesnakes, cobras, vipers and other venomous native species (60 in all) are kept here. You can observe them in safety and also meet lizards, turtles and snakes collected from around the world. Visitors can watch the snakes being milked of their venom at 11am, 2pm and 5pm each day.
Location: 19 miles southeast of Old Town. 5705 East Irlo Bronson Memorial Highway, St Cloud. Tel: (407) 892–6905. Open: Tuesday to Sunday 9am–5.30pm. Admission charge.

GREEN MEADOWS FARM

When the children want to meet something more cuddly than an alligator, this is the place to head for. There are pony rides and tractor-drawn hayrides and a whole gaggle of farmyard animals to milk, pet, chase and learn about.
Location: 6 miles east of Old Town. Take I–4 exit 25A/US192 east to Poinciana Boulevard, turn right, continue for 5 miles. Open: daily 9.30am–5pm. Admission charge.

THE HAUNTED HOUSE AT OLD TOWN

Following the success of Terror on Church Street (see page 139) another haunted house, with actors taking the part of fictional monsters, has opened to scare the holidaymakers in Kissimmee.
Location: Old Town (see below). Tel: (407) 397–2231. Open: Monday to Thursday 10am–10pm. Admission charge.

OLD TOWN

Signposted by its giant Ferris wheel, the turn-of-the-century themed Old Town shopping mall has a delightfully ornate vintage fairground carousel and some 70

KISSIMMEE COWBOYS

Yes, Florida did have cowboys (they called themselves 'cow hunters') and they weren't so different from their more famous western counterparts. They had roundups, went on long cattle drives, tried to stop rustlers and experienced their own share of a hard and sometimes violent lifestyle. There were some differences, however, in part due to the nature of the terrain. The marshes, hammocks (raised areas of hardwood vegetation), and pine woods of the state prevented them using the lariot which was perfectly suited to the open range. Instead Florida cowboys used trained dogs and whips (from where the name 'Cracker' may have derived) to drive their cattle. Their small lean 'scrub cows' were descended from the same ancestor as the famous Texas longhorns – Spanish cattle from Andalucia.

Cows were rounded up and branded each spring in what were termed 'cow camps'. These comprised a simple holding pen for the cattle and a crude shelter for the men. They were constructed at regular intervals along the routes of the cattle drive to the west coast from where the cows were shipped south to Cuba.

You can see a reconstructed 1876 cow camp at Lake Kissimmee State Park (see page 125). It is open on weekends and public holidays from 9.30am to 4.30pm.

To see todays' cowboys (and cowgirls) at play visit the Kissimmee Rodeo where you can enjoy displays of calf-roping, bareback riding, bull riding, steer wrestling and barrel racing. It takes place every Friday from 8pm at the Kissimmee Sports Arena on South Hoagland Boulevard, 2 miles south of US 192 (tel: (407) 933–0022).

It's a small world! Looking down on the Summer Palace at Splendid China

SPLENDID CHINA

Florida's latest theme park is a brilliant evocation of 5,000 years of China in miniature. It was inspired by the original Splendid China park in Shenzen, China and is a highly crafted authentic reproduction of the country's great sights.

The entrance to the park, however, starts Disney-fashion with a full-size reconstruction of a typical main street from the past – in this case dating from around AD1400. It is crafted from solid wood and is made entirely without the use of nails.

There are over 60 splendid monuments to pore over, plus a full-scale reproduction of Suzhou Gardens. The Great Wall is, of course, the most famous landmark, painstakingly constructed from some 6 million two-inch long bricks, individually laid by a team of Chinese artisans. The real Wall

stretches for 2,150 miles; this one is a half-mile long.

Another highlight is the 9,999 rooms of the Imperial Palace in the Forbidden City, reproduced stone by stone, tile by tile, right down to the slightest detail. Other wonders in miniature include the fantastic limestone peaks of the Stone Forest of Yunan, the fabled Terracotta Army, the White Pagoda, the Temple of Confucius and the Leshan Grand Buddha. In all, the park covers an area of 76 acres – no small undertaking.

There's also a stunning film to watch, plus demonstrations of acrobatics, Mongolian wrestling, Chinese ballet and martial arts featuring 150 of China's very best entertainers.

The food at the restaurants here puts most theme park catering to shame (take-aways are also available) and the shops too are worth a visit.

Location: 3 miles west of I–4 exit 25B off

US 192. Splendid China Boulevard, Kissimmee. Tel: (407) 396–7111. Open: daily 10am–10pm. Admission charge.

TUPPERWARE WORLD HEADQUARTERS

This isn't a factory tour, though a film does show you the manufacturing process. The full range of Tupperware products are on show, together with a history of food containers that dates back to ancient Egyptian times.
Location: 15 miles northeast of Old Town. South Orange Blossom Trail (US 441 South), Kissimmee. Tel: (407) 847–3111. Open: Monday to Friday 9am–4pm. Free.

WATER MANIA

An all-action water park (see page 87).

A WORLD OF ORCHIDS

This pristine new attraction is housed in state-of-the-art, climate-controlled glass conservatories, including a tropical rain forest setting. It is claimed to be the world's largest permanent exhibition of rare and exotic orchids in flower at any one time. There are over 2,000 specimens from around the globe. If you

> **WHAT'S IN A NAME?**
> Kissimmee (pronounced Kiss-SIM-me) is, like many of Florida's exotic sounding place names, of Indian origin. It means Heaven's Place.

can't bear to leave them behind, many species can be mailed on to you at home.
Location: 4 miles west of Old Town. 2501 N Old Lake Wilson Road, Kissimmee. Tel: (407) 396–1887. Open: daily 10am–6pm. Admission charge.

XANADU – HOME OF THE FUTURE

Tomorrow's domestic world – a futuristic vision of how we might all be living during the next century. This 15-bedroom house is full of bright new ideas and computer-controlled gadgetry to take the drudgery out of home life.
Location: 6 miles east of Old Town. 4800 Irlo Bronson Memorial Highway. Tel: (407) 396–1992. Open: 10am–10pm. Admission charge.

Colourful blooms at World of Orchids

IMAGINEERING

The collection of magical special effects that allows you to enter another world in the theme parks is encapsulated in the Walt Disney term, 'Imagineering'. This applies equally to low-technology rides as it does to the latest film and sound techniques. Low-tech does not mean low thrills however. Disney's Space Mountain, for instance, is the simple but brilliant concept of a roller-coaster in the dark. This idea has subsequently been applied to water-chute rides – both applications provide some of the most heart-stopping moments in Orlando!

Thanks to the 'imagineers' of Orlando the physical confines of mechanical rides have been opened out by simulators, 3-D vision, CircleVision, audio-animatronics (life-like robots) and holograms. You will come across all of these clever techniques as you tour the parks.

The most incredible simulator ride of all is Universal Studios' Back to the Future, where your 'De Lorean motor car' flies through a hair-raising landscape and even solid objects (you can't help but raise your hands to protect yourself!). All this activity is actually being projected on to a seven-storey-high hemispherical screen,

though you, of course, are totally unaware of this device – your senses completely fooled by the technology. To enhance the sensations of sudden and violent movement, powerful hydraulics make your car lurch and twist and rise and fall, though in reality the movements

are only a fraction of those that you feel in the simulated screen world in front of you.

For the best examples of 3-D Vision visit Universal Studios' Alfred Hitchcock 3-D Theater or Disney–MGM's 3-D Muppet Vision. Both of these are film theatre presentations, rather than simulator rides, but will still have you ducking and dodging as objects seem to fly out of the screen right towards you.

The gentlest simulator-type attraction is CircleVision film. This is a technique whereby a number of projectors and screens either completely surround the audience (360-degree CircleVision), or partially surround them (less than 360-degree). The effect is to place the viewer almost in the middle of a three-dimensional scene. To all intents and purposes you are actually flying or boating or travelling by dog-sled through the US, Canada, France, China or wherever else in the world. You can see in front, to the left, to the right and even behind. With 360-degree CircleVision the audience actually remain standing, next to lean-rails, so they can turn around and see all sides of the action.

Walt Disney have been pioneering animatronics (wax robots) and audio-animatronics (speaking or sound-making robots) for many years now and the standards get better and better. The very best is Epcot's American Adventure where long-gone American heroes still look and sound uncannily alive.

Universal Studios

*I*t was Universal Studios (Hollywood) who in 1966 pioneered the concept of taking the general public behind the silver screen, to see how movies were made. Eventually this led Universal to develop the first ever film theme park.

The company announced that its second park was to open in Orlando in 1990, but were narrowly beaten to the opening date by the Disney–MGM park. Beginnings were not auspicious, with technical problems bedevilling the park in its early days. Now, however, there are many who prefer Universal to Disney–MGM and it has established itself alongside Sea World as Orlando's second major attraction. The park is large and you need two days to see everything in comfort.

The world of movie-making, according to Universal Studios

THE RIDES
BACK TO THE FUTURE ... THE RIDE

The greatest simulator ride on earth takes you on an enthralling chase based on the film *Back to the Future II*. They say the ride cost more to make than the film. The difference is that you only watched the film – there's never any doubt that you are actually part of the ride. Look out for that dinosaur! For many visitors this attraction alone is worth the entrance fee.

EARTHQUAKE – THE BIG ONE

All the drama of a major earthquake becomes reality as a subway station in the San Francisco area of the backlot is destroyed in an enactment of a scene from *Earthquake*, the disaster movie. As the 'quake hits 8.3 on the Richter scale

DISNEY–MGM OR UNIVERSAL?

As a first-time visitor to Orlando you are faced with a difficult choice. You probably won't have the time, the money or the inclination to see two film-theme parks in the same holiday, so which one should you choose? Universal is much larger, arguably more 'realistic' and a little less commercial than Disney–MGM. Disney–MGM, however, has that obvious but priceless commodity – Disney films, which take every parent back to their own childhood and bring to life current children's favourites. Universal may claim the best rides but Disney is higher on charm and offers an excellent behind-the-scenes tour. The combination Walt Disney World ticket also offers good value for money for Disney–MGM guests.

your train bucks and pitches violently. There are some great pyrotechnic effects as electric cables ignite gas mains and, while waiting for the ride, you will already have seen a fascinating audience participation demonstration of how such scenes are created.

ET ADVENTURE

Younger children and their parents will find this ride through the night sky totally enchanting even if teenagers will rate it as rather tame. The special effects add a dreamlike quality to it all, but it's not exactly a thrill a minute.

FUNTASTIC WORLD OF HANNA-BARBERA

A splendid high-speed simulator ride which makes the most of some great cartoon effects – starring the Flintstones, Scooby Doo, Dick Dastardly and Muttley and lots of other favourites on a chase which will shake you all over.

UNIVERSAL STUDIOS

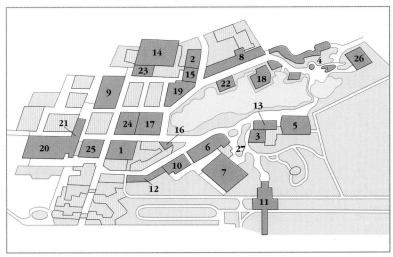

1 Alfred Hitchcock: The Art of Making Movies
2 An American Tail Theater
3 Animal Actors Stage
4 Amity and Jaws
5 Back to the Future ... The Ride
6 Café La Bamba
7 ET Adventure
8 Earthquake – The Big One
9 Ghostbusters
10 Gory, Gruesome &

Grotesque Horror Make-up Show
11 Hard Rock Café
12 Hollywood Boulevard
13 International Food Bazaar
14 Kongfrontation
15 Louie's Italian Restaurant
16 Mel's Drive-In
17 Murder, She Wrote! Mystery Theater
18 New England
19 New York Street Sets

20 Nickolodeon Studios
21 Production Studio Tour
22 San Francisco/Fisherman's Wharf
23 Screen Test Home Video Adventure
24 Studio Stars Restaurant
25 The Funtastic World of Hanna-Barbera
26 Wild, Wild, Wild West Stunt Show
27 World Expo

and fro above the East River. Standing five-storeys tall and weighing in at six tons, the fearsome Kong is the largest animatronic model ever built. Full-scale helicopters and dramatic sound tracks add to the effect – and you can relive it all on a video playback.

OTHER ATTRACTIONS
ALFRED HITCHCOCK – THE ART OF MAKING MOVIES
Watch the classic scenes from *The Birds* in 3-D surround-vision. It's so scarily realistic you end up looking for droppings on your shoulder! Anthony Perkins narrates an account of how *Psycho* was made and pleads innocence of the crime – he was rehearsing on

JAWS!
Just when you thought it was safe to go back into the theme park, the savage denizen of the deep returns with a vengeance. What started life as a pretty tame trolley ride at the original Universal Studios in Hollywood has been developed into one of the best adventures in all Orlando, greatly helped along by the realistic Amity harbour New England waterfront re-creation. Board the boat and anticipate the first sighting of the 32-foot long shark – it is still bound to catch you by surprise! Be prepared for a soaking and for the wall of flame which almost literally sears the back of your neck.

KONGFRONTATION
Yes, he is still dangling from the Empire State Building and on this ride you are one of his potential victims, trapped in a tramway car which the gorilla swings to

Broadway when a stand-in played the shadowy figure with the knife at the Bates Motel. Oh, and it was chocolate syrup, not blood, that swirled down the plughole.

ANIMAL ACTORS STAGE

An entertaining and informative show which explains how moviemakers train their animal stars, and then gives the four-legged actors the chance to go through their paces.

DYNAMITE NIGHTS STUNT SPECTACULAR

An all-action end to the day, with a *Miami Vice*-inspired boat chase round the lagoon. Pick your spot early (the footbridge at the other end of the lagoon on New York's South Street is a good place) as there are few points where you can see more than a snatch of the waterborne action.

Crooners at Mel's Drive-In

FRONT LOT

Shops, restaurants, the Plaza of the Stars, and a reproduction of the American diner from *The Last Picture Show*, with classic 'Yank-mobiles' outside.

Somewhere in these waters a big surprise is in store for you!

Plan your day carefully, there's a lot to see and not enough time to see it in

GHOSTBUSTERS

Ghostbusters is a smash with fans of green gloop and has some clever special effects. If ghost-busting is your scene you'll probably love it. Otherwise give it a miss if you're pushed for time.

HARD ROCK CAFÉ

The Orlando branch of the famous rock 'n' roll food chain. You can eat here without paying admission to the theme park – there's a separate entrance off the street (see pages 158–9).

HOLLYWOOD BOULEVARD

Browse along the Sunset Boulevard and Beverly Hills sets and shops, then get made up as a monster (or even a Munster) at the Gory, Gruesome and Grotesque Horror Make-Up Show.

Coming soon! Chills and thrills from
the Jurassic era

MURDER, SHE WROTE!
MYSTERY THEATER

Visitors can try their hand at the
producer's role in movie-making after
Angela Lansbury (on film) explains how
it's all done, with an episode from her
popular TV crime series.

NEW YORK STREET SETS

Contained within two blocks are all the
sights of New York, faithfully reproduced
to a high standard of craftsmanship.
There's a New York Irish bar, complete
with etched glass windows, and an
Italian restaurant, as well as lots of street
theatre – with characters like WC Fields,
the Blues Brothers and Charlie Chaplin
passing by.

NICKELODEON STUDIOS

Visit the set where the popular American
kids-TV show is produced. You can, by
advance application, arrange for your
own children to be in the audience or
even to take part. Tel: (407) 363–3770
for details.

Other Universal attractions include
Fievel's Playland (based on *An American
Tail*), the Wild, Wild, Wild West Stunt
Show and Beetlejuice's Graveyard Revue.

Location: 1000 Universal Studios Plaza,
Orlando. Tel: (407) 363–8000.
Open: 9.30am (closing dates vary
according to season).
Admission charge.

A CAST OF THOUSANDS

The Peabody Orlando, one of the world's most luxurious hotels, has five especially pampered long-term guests. Each day at 11am, the red carpet is literally rolled out across the vast and luxurious lobby. The lift descends from the hotel's recreation level and, to the tune of *King Cotton March*, five ducks waddle across to the fountain, which they enter via a special portable staircase.

At 5pm prompt, the reverse process is followed and, having spent the afternoon swimming in the fountain, the ducks return to their exclusive Royal Duck Palace where fresh water runs from brass fountains into a black marble pool. The 'palace' even has a ceiling fan for hot summer nights. It is all a tradition which began at the Peabody's sister hotel in Memphis in the 1930s.

Melanie Moorman is the Peabody Orlando's first female duck master, fully schooled in breeding, nutrition, and the importance of pecking order in training and motivating the ducks.

Orlando is brim-full with oddball jobs like Melanie's and the colourful characters who carry them out. Lookalikes are especially in demand. At Universal Studios the familiar figure of Charlie Chaplin can be seen walking down the street twiddling his cane as WC Fields drives past at the wheel of

There's a host of stars and famous faces at this Studio call

Peabody Ducks, King John at Disney-MGM, ET at Universal Studios

Miami Vice.
Officially, there is only one Mickey Mouse. In truth, a whole team of actors don costumes to entertain the kids in the guise of Mickey, Donald Duck, Goofy and all the other much-loved Disney characters.

These people are all part of the cast of thousands who help turn a visit to Orlando into the experience of a lifetime.

his vintage Model T Ford. And around the corner the Blues Brothers are busy entertaining with help from a lady who looks and sounds just like the real Aretha Franklin. Meanwhile aspiring Hollywood stunt men learn their craft by enacting a speedboat chase à la

Sea World

Sea World of Florida is the world's largest and most popular marine-life park. It is a major theme park in every sense, beautifully laid out around 135 acres of manicured grounds and pools and recently it has even added its first thrill ride. But the stars in this aquatic zoo world are neither the special effects nor are they celluloid fantasies: they are the creatures of the deep. Allow a full day to see it all, but if you run out of time cash in your day ticket for a two-day pass (before you leave) which for a little more will allow you another day.

CARIBBEAN TIDE POOL/COMMUNITY POOL

If you've ever wanted to touch a dolphin, pat a sea-lion or even stroke a stingray, here is your chance. You can even buy snacks to feed them. It may sound a little strange but it's a great favourite.

HOTEL CLYDE AND SEAMORE

This is an amusing comedy-with-a-conservation showcase for the talents of the park's best double acts, sea-lions Clyde and Seamore. Otters and walruses get bit parts in a show which is great fun for all the family.

SEA WORLD

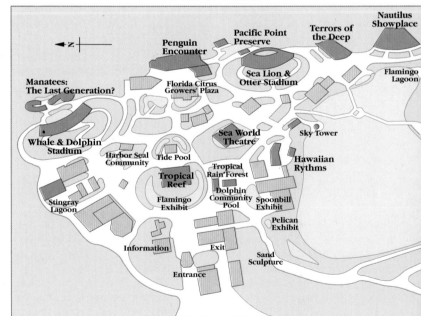

A killer whale welcome to the park

Clydesdale Hamlet

Anheuser-Busch Hospitality Center

Radio Control Boats & Trucks

Shamu Stadium

Shamu's Happy Harbor

Mission: Bermuda Triangle

Atlantis Water Ski Stadium

Special Events Pavilion

BEHIND THE SCENES

Sea World provides three opportunities for you to see what goes on backstage and to fully appreciate the park's conservation and rehabilitation programmes; over the years it has responded to more than a thousand distress calls, aiding ill, injured or orphaned manatees, whales, dolphins, otters, sea turtles and waterfowl. The most comprehensive is the 90-minute Backstage Exploration Tour (additional charge). Animal Training Discoveries is a fascinating 45-minute film which unveils the secrets behind the park's animal training techniques. Window to the Sea is another inspiring film, going backstage at Shamu Stadium and out into the field with Sea World's research crew.

Fascinating underwater exhibit brings all the drama and action of the sea to you

MANATEES: THE LAST GENERATION?

Visitors enter Sea World's latest conservation attraction via the Manatee Theater. This immerses the viewer in an excellent state-of-the-art multi-plane presentation of the manatee's world, using underwater footage shot from the manatee's perspective.

Next is a brilliant three-acre wide river and lagoon reconstruction, home to manatees and hundreds of native fish. A 126-foot long acrylic panel provides underwater views. There is also a nursing pool specially built for manatee mothers and babies and an informative beached animals rescue station display.

The attraction continues with a 27,000-gallon marsh area, home to huge

American alligators, and also features an area for native birds. Here wood storks, great egrets, white ibises, green herons and other species may be seen.

PACIFIC POINT PRESERVE

A slice of the rocky northern Pacific coast has been ingeniously transferred to this corner of Florida to show visitors Californian sea-lions and harbour and fur seals frolicking in an impressive and totally convincing near-natural setting. The stonework has been meticulously crafted and moulded from actual Pacific coastal stone and provides the seals and sea-lions with perches for sunning and cliffs for diving. Also featured are underwater ledges, beaches and grottos. The whole habitat has been filled with

Right: sea captains hats for sale

450,000 gallons of seawater, which is whipped up to two-foot high waves. Underwater viewing panels put guests face to whiskered face and feeding times are always extremely popular.

PENGUIN ENCOUNTER
When it's baking outside this is the place to be – it even snows inside here! This refrigerated Antarctic ice box, secure behind plexiglass, is home to over 200 penguins, representing some 17 species. It's brilliantly presented with moving walkways providing above- and below-water views. Not surprisingly it's a very popular attraction.

Below: Californian sea-lions at Pacific Point Preserve

Shamu's Happy Harbor – a shipload of fun and games for the children

SHAMU'S HAPPY HARBOR

When the kids need to let off steam, bring them to this huge play area. There's a schooner funship with water cannons to drench their friends, a water maze, a ball crawl and a towering four-storey net climb and tower.

SHAMU STADIUM BREEDING AND RESEARCH POOL

Sea World are famous for breeding killer whales and the video of baby Namu's dramatic birth is played on screens throughout the complex. Here you can see the world's largest nursery and enjoy unparalleled underwater viewing of these magnificent creatures.

SHAMU: NEW VISIONS

This is quite literally the big one. Shamu and her offspring, baby Shamu (born September 1993) and Namu (born December 1993) cavort and jump effortlessly in their 5-million-gallon plexiglass tank while enthusiastic youngsters sit in the front rows to get a thorough soaking when the whales hit the water. You will also learn about the facts and folklore of killer whales and see how Sea World care for these gargantuan creatures. The evening show, Shamu Night Magic, is even more spectacular.

SKY TOWER

Jump aboard the tower lift for one of the best views over Central Orlando (additional charge).

TERRORS OF THE DEEP

In a clever role reversal it is the spectators who are in the glass bowl (actually plexiglass tubes) while around them swim sharks, barracuda and menacing fish of all kinds.

TROPICAL REEF
Another of Sea World's brilliant re-creations, this features over 1,000 tropical fish, many in breathtaking shapes and colours, in a giant coral reef tank.

WHALE AND DOLPHIN STADIUM
A sympathetic and engaging show which features bottle-nose dolphins and false killer whales. As well as the usual tricks the audience gains an insight into these gentle, intelligent creatures.

Round your day off with a free beer at the Anheuser Busch Hospitality Center

and see the famous Clydesdale horses which pull the traditional brewery delivery wagons.

Location: Intersection of I–4 and Bee-Line Expressway, Sea World Drive. Tel: (407) 351–3600. Open: daily 9am–7pm (later at peak times). Admission charge.

Watch the dolphins work out

KILLERS AT LARGE

The killer whale shows at Sea World are almost by definition the biggest and most spectacular wildlife shows on earth. It is therefore not surprising that they also generate a good deal of controversy. Some ecologists (and many members of the general public) believe it is inherently cruel to keep such creatures in captivity and to exploit them as a form of entertainment. Sea World, however, has some potent counter arguments.

Much of what the scientific community knows about killer whales has come from the work of Sea World. Furthermore, studies show that living in captivity, in reputable establishments like Sea World, does not reduce the whales' life-span (which is 25 to 35 years). Whether the animals are happy or not is of course open to conjecture. However, they certainly don't appear to be unhappy. Behaviour patterns at Sea World closely follow those in the wild and the fact that they reproduce successfully in captivity indicates that they are at least comfortable in their surroundings. In fact Sea World has bred six babies since 1985, making it the most successful establishment in the world in this field.

None of Sea World's stars are ever forced to perform, nor are they punished for not

Yesterday's villains, today's stars

performing. Positive reinforcement (ie a system of rewards) is used in the training methods only to encourage extensions of the animal's natural behaviour. Critics of course would ask where natural behaviour ends and artifical behaviour (for the delight of the crowd) begins.

Finally, argues Sea World, marine life theme parks are the best way of educating the public. Years ago killer whales were misunderstood, feared and hunted. Today there is widespread public support and con-cern for wildlife preservation.

Walt Disney World

Walt Disney World is quite unlike any other place you will ever have experienced. There is so much to see and do within the different theme parks that if you have not made at least a basic plan of action, you are likely to end up confused and, at the end of the day, frustrated at what you have missed. Admission is expensive (a one-day ticket during 1994 for two adults and two children aged 3 to 10 cost $126 excluding tax) so it's only sensible to get the very best value for your money.

All aboard the magic bus!

WHEN TO GO

The least crowded seasons are January through the first week in February, September through November (except Thanksgiving weekend) and from Thanskgiving to the beginning of the Christmas vacation. Post-Easter through early June is also a relatively light season. Although there is a special magic to Walt Disney World at Christmas, it is not worth making your first trip at this or any other peak period if you want to avoid very long queues. However, even at the quieter times you will still encounter lengthy waits for the more popular attractions.

TICKETS (PASSES)

As far as the average holidaymaker is concerned there is a choice of three types of ticket.

One-day tickets are valid for one major park (Magic Kingdom, Epcot or Disney–MGM). All major parks cost the same. There are no two- or three-day tickets, so if you want to visit more than one park you have to buy tickets individually, or invest in a four-day or five-day pass. These give one day at each of the three parks with an extra day or two days to return to the parks. There are no restrictions on which four or five days you can visit, these need not be consecutive, nor do you have to specify dates in advance.

There is no difference in the price of tickets, whether you are staying within Walt Disney World or not. However, only residents are allowed to visit more than one park in a day. Another bonus afforded to residents (and to four- and five-day pass holders) is the provision of free transportation within the World – other 'guests' pay a flat rate, around $2.50 per day.

The five-day pass has the added bonus of including free admission to Walt Disney World's other four admission-paying 'minor' parks (Typhoon Lagoon, River Country, Discovery Island and Pleasure Island) for up to seven days from the day the pass is first used.

So which pass should you buy? The answer depends on how much you want to see. The price structure is such that it is only slightly cheaper to visit all three

WALT DISNEY WORLD

Map of Walt Disney World showing locations including Lake Reams, Lake Mabel, Lake Sheen, Magic Kingdom, Contemporary Resort, Sotub Lake, Pocket Lake, Big Sand Lake, Orlando, Airport, Exit 28, Reedy Lake, Seven Seas Lagoon, Bay Lake, Discovery Island, Osprey Ridge Golf Course, Grand Floridian Beach Resort, Magnolia Golf Course, Pioneer Hall, River Country, Grand Cypress Golf Club, Sea World, Disney Inn, Monorail Station, Palm Golf Course, Polynesian Resort, Fort Wilderness, Eagle Pines Golf Course, Vineland, Bay Lake, Lake Buena Vista, The Crossroads of Lake Buena Vista, Lake Buena Vista Golf Club, EPCOT Center, Spaceship Earth, Disney's Village Resort, Exit 27, Disney Village Marketplace, World Showcase, WDW Swan, WDW Dolphin, Pleasure Island, Typhoon Lagoon, Lake Bryan, EASTERN BELTWAY, Caribbean Beach Resort, Exit 26, Disney-MGM Studios Theme Park, Reedy Creek, Bonnet Creek, Kissimmee, Exit 25.

major parks individually, than to buy a four-day ticket, so for a little more money you get an extra day. And as you need a minimum of four days to see everything this option is recommended. The difference between the price of a four-day and a five-day ticket is (approximately) equivalent to the admission price of three of the four 'minor' parks. So, if you intend visiting the three major parks, plus three (or all) of the 'minor' parks, buy the five-day pass and it will actually save you money as well as giving you one or two extra days to return to the major parks.

Don't worry if three-quarters of the way through the day you realise you should have bought a longer duration

ticket. Just return to the ticket office before the end of the day and you can cash in your current ticket against a new one with no penalty charge.

Children's discounts (typically 20 per cent less than adult price) apply to age group 3 to 9. Children aged under three are admitted free. Take a birth certificate copy if there is any doubt.

OPENING HOURS

Check these with Walt Disney before you go (see below), then re-confirm when you are in Orlando. All parks are open daily (Typhoon Lagoon and River Country close for renovation during winter) with extended hours in summer and during holiday periods.

Heaven's gate – welcome to the Magic Kingdom

HOW TO BEAT THE CROWDS

Every Disney veteran has his or her own strategy and reams upon reams are devoted to this subject, but as you are on holiday, rather than conducting a precision military exercise, just remember the following tips:

Always get to the major theme parks at least 30 minutes before the stated opening times (the gates open 30 or sometimes even 60 minutes before then) and head straight for the attractions with the longest queuing times.

Pick your way back to the entrance, choosing the rides with the smallest queues. If you miss a ride go back to it as late as possible in the day (when less determined visitors will have gone home) or during one of the parades which will inevitably distract attention. The only problem is that the parades are also well worth seeing! For parade times and details call at the main information desks.

TAKING A BREAK

If you want to leave the park, just get your hand stamped and you can return on the same day at no extra charge. Discovery Island is the perfect place for a spot of peace (though there is an additional admission charge unless you have a five-day pass).

IN LINE FOR THE BIG ONES

The attractions which usually have the most time-consuming queues are as follows: Magic Kingdom – Space Mountain, Pirates of the Caribbean, Jungle Cruise, Splash Mountain, Big Thunder Mountain Railroad; Epcot – Spaceship Earth, Living Seas, The Land, Journey into Imagination Ride; Disney–MGM – Body Tours, The Great Movie Ride, The Backstage Tour, Muppet Vision 3-D, Star Wars, Twilight Zone of Terror.

Helpful individual notice boards (near the entrances to all popular rides and shows) inform you approximately how long you have to wait, based on your current position in the queue. Central notice boards are also constantly updated, telling you which attractions are currently full and which are empty.

FURTHER INFORMATION

Before you go contact Guest Services, Walt Disney World, PO Box 10040, Lake Buena Vista, FL 32830–0040. For information tel: (407) 824–4321.

Measuring up for Thunder Mountain

DISABLED VISITORS

Walt Disney World publish a handy *Guidebook For Disabled Guests* which describes special facilities and gives useful tips. Designated parking areas are available, as well as transport adapted to lift and carry wheelchairs.

WALT DISNEY'S DREAM

Walt Disney was a remarkable man who created a multi-billion dollar industry which today attracts many millions of visitors to its theme parks in California, Florida, Japan and France.

It was the ever-popular cartoon character, Mickey Mouse, who first brought fame to this peerless creative genius, with Minnie Mouse, Donald Duck, Pluto, Goofy and all the rest soon following from his inspired pen and brush. The cartoon spectacular, *Fantasia*, released shortly before the outbreak of World War II, first revealed the impressive scale of Walter Elias Disney's kaleidoscopic imagination and, when peace returned, he embarked on his most ambitious ever project – creating a theme park which would bring a whole new dimension to the world of entertainment.

Disneyland, located in Los Angeles, quickly established itself as the world's greatest popular entertainment centre, its rides and attractions bringing many of Disney's favourite characters to life. And though Disney dominated the industry, rivals soon sprang up.

The fact that these competitors did not hurt Disney's own ever-increasing admissions, proved to Walt that demand was seemingly insatiable. But to capitalise on that demand, he needed room for expansion – and room was one thing which southern California, with its rapidly rising land costs, could not offer him.

At that time, Orlando was already

starting to enjoy a boom. Its weather was good, its location convenient, and in 1965, without letting outsiders get wind of his dreams, Walt Disney discretely bought a huge tract of

The maestro –
Walt Disney
Inset: Walt with
Mickey Mouse,
at Disneyland

seemingly near-worthless land at a bargain price. The construction teams moved in almost immediately.

Sadly, this visionary man was already suffering from terminal cancer. He carried on mapping out his ideas in his hospital bedroom right up till his death at the age of 65.

Walt's brother and partner, Roy, had argued consistently against the grandiose scheme, but now he took up the blueprint and masterminded it through to completion, insisting that the new dreamland be called Walt Disney World in tribute to its creator.

The Magic Kingdom

*W*ith its spires and turrets straight out of a fairy-tale fantasy, Cinderella's Castle ranks alongside the Eiffel Tower, the Taj Mahal and Big Ben as one of the world's most instantly recognisable landmarks. Indeed, for many, it is as familiar and as potent a symbol as the profile of Mickey Mouse himself. Not that the structure is unique, for the castle, like the rest of Magic Kingdom, closely replicates the original Disneyland in California. In Orlando, it is all simply on a bigger and more expansive scale, with the park covering some 100 acres and featuring over 50 major rides and attractions.

Even reaching the Magic Kingdom is something of an adventure, for once having parked and negotiated the pay booths, you still have a way to go, making the journey either by monorail, or by ferry across the Seven Seas Lagoon, which provides the most romantic view of the castle.

The dream-like quality of it all evaporates somewhat when you get close up and the fake nature of the structures becomes increasingly apparent. Children, however, will continue to see it all as a true wonderland.

The Magic Kingdom is divided into seven distinct 'lands', each running off Central Plaza, which connects Cinderella's Castle and Main Street USA. Endless shops, eating places, sideshows and other diversions, from street entertainment to the chance to pose for pictures with Mickey and his famous chums, all make for an action-packed day. Smaller children often find it all a bit overwhelming.

Instantly recognisable – Cinderella's Castle

High-tech transport: Magic Kingdom monorail

Return to a slower pace of life on Main Street USA

MAIN STREET USA

Everyone's idealised memory of small town USA as it once was (or perhaps never was). Actually, it's an excuse for merchandising, being packed full of all-too-tempting shops. City Hall provides a useful information centre and rides are available in horse-drawn buggies and vintage fire engines.

PENNY ARCADE

A slot machine heaven and it's all vintage mechanical devices, rather than today's computerised video wizardry.

MAIN STREET CINEMA

Given such a wonderful back catalogue of classic movies and cartoon shorts, Disney are never short of something entertaining to screen here.

Don't miss the highly colourful and popular Main Street parades

THE WALT DISNEY STORY

The great man himself, recalling just how it all came about, via a fitting testament to a life he spent in the service of kids of all ages. The Hall of Fame here is packed full of the *memorabilia* of a wonderful life and includes letters of admiration from presidents and royalty.

MAGIC KINGDOM

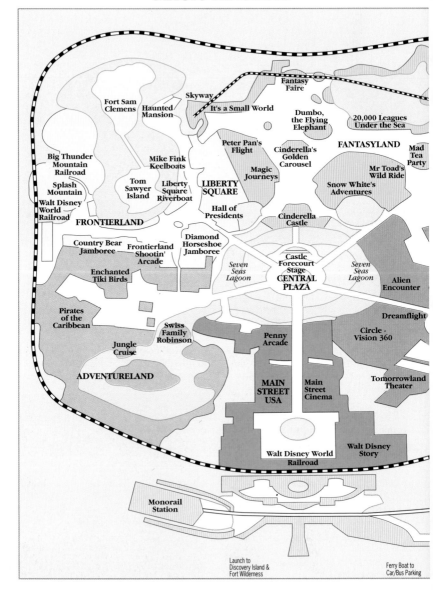

Fort Sam Clemens

Haunted Mansion

Skyway

It's a Small World

Fantasy Faire

Dumbo, the Flying Elephant

20,000 Leagues Under the Sea

Big Thunder Mountain Railroad

Mike Fink Keelboats

Peter Pan's Flight

Cinderella's Golden Carousel

FANTASYLAND

Mad Tea Party

Splash Mountain

Walt Disney World Railroad

Tom Sawyer Island

Liberty Square Riverboat

Magic Journeys

LIBERTY SQUARE

Mr Toad's Wild Ride

Snow White's Adventures

FRONTIERLAND

Hall of Presidents

Cinderella Castle

Country Bear Jamboree

Frontierland Shootin' Arcade

Diamond Horseshoe Jamboree

Castle Forecourt Stage

Enchanted Tiki Birds

Seven Seas Lagoon

CENTRAL PLAZA

Seven Seas Lagoon

Alien Encounter

Pirates of the Caribbean

Dreamflight

Swiss Family Robinson

Penny Arcade

Circle - Vision 360

Jungle Cruise

ADVENTURELAND

MAIN STREET USA

Main Street Cinema

Tomorrowland Theater

Walt Disney World Railroad

Walt Disney Story

Monorail Station

Launch to Discovery Island & Fort Wilderness

Ferry Boat to Car/Bus Parking

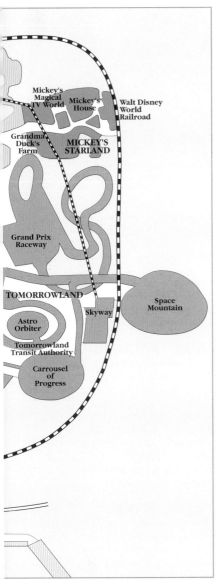

Mickey's
Magical
TV World · Mickey's
House · Walt Disney
World
Railroad

Grandma
Duck's
Farm · **MICKEY'S
STARLAND**

Grand Prix
Raceway

TOMORROWLAND

Skyway · Space
Mountain

Astro
Orbiter

Tomorrowland
Transit Authority

Carrousel
of
Progress

ADVENTURELAND

The tropical setting here evokes the world of the great explorers, with suitably themed rides and attractions.

ENCHANTED TIKI BIRDS

An old-fashioned and twee attraction replete with animated birds in a tropical thatched hut setting. One of Disney's few very missable attractions.

JUNGLE CRUISE

Ten minutes of pure fantasy on a dreamy ride which recreates the Asian jungle, the Nile Valley and the Amazonian rain-forest. Along the way you'll meet animals, all in audio-animatronic form (robots which make life-like sounds).

PIRATES OF THE CARIBBEAN

A favourite cruise ride with brilliant special effects which create a jokey skull and crossbones adventure.

SWISS FAMILY ROBINSON

The shipwrecked family's island home is pretty convincingly reconstructed and is lots of fun as you clamber about amid all the tropical (plastic) foliage.

A host of Minnie Mice (and friend)

Roller coasting: on land with Big Thunder Mountain; on water with Splash Mountain

FRONTIERLAND
BIG THUNDER MOUNTAIN RAILROAD
This three-minute rollercoaster ride through an old mining tunnel may be tame by the latest thrill-ride standards, but is still worth queuing for.

COUNTRY BEAR JAMBOREE
A typically Disneyesque stage show featuring fun from the American backwoods with animated bears and an excess of corn.

DIAMOND HORSESHOE JAMBOREE
High-kicking dance-hall gals and high-spirited cowboys create a Wild West saloon extravaganza. Booking is required – just apply at the attraction itself.

TOM SAWYER ISLAND
An evocative reconstruction of the adventures of Tom and his chum Huckleberry Finn, reached, appropriately enough, by raft ride.

SPLASH MOUNTAIN
This hair-raising log flume ride reaches speeds of up to 40mph and culminates in a five-storey plunge!

LIBERTY SQUARE
Visit old-time New England and capture the mood of Revolutionary days – with Paul Revere, the Minute Men, the Boston Tea Party and so on.

HALL OF PRESIDENTS
A somewhat chauvinistic exercise with various past presidents (in animatronic form) waving the Stars and Stripes. (Children may be less impressed.)

HAUNTED MANSION
Disney's entertaining and light-hearted version of the classic fairground ghost train ride provides at least one very memorable special effect. Great for funfair traditionalists.

FANTASYLAND

This is the Magic Kingdom's prime magnet for younger guests, and is Orlando's closest thing to a traditional fairground, with such sweet and innocent old-fashioned rides as the Mad Hatter's Tea Party and Dumbo The Flying Elephant.

IT'S A SMALL WORLD

A seemingly interminable boat ride through elaborately devised miniature sets depicting various parts of the world in schmaltzy terms. Young ones love it!

LEGEND OF THE LION KING

Disney's newest animated motion picture musical is brought to life as a spectacular live theatre production, using a new kind of 'living-animation'. Disney's Humanimals are larger-than-life-size figures that look just like their animated film counterparts. They are manipulated by human 'animateers', hidden below stage level. The stage is transformed too by special effects and as thousands of wildebeests come charging forward, there is some panic in the front rows!

MAGIC JOURNEYS

This 3-D film show is slim on plot, but exceedingly good on special effects.

20,000 LEAGUES UNDER THE SEA

This long-standing and rather staid ride is still popular with visitors wishing to explore the simulated 'deep' in mock-up Captain Nemo submarines.

Shaken, stirred and submerged; Mad Hatter teacups and Captain Nemo's submarine

Mickey's Starland show; quiet before the storm outside Space Mountain

TOMORROWLAND

A profusion of futuristic rides with Space Mountain standing head and shoulders among some pretty dull fare. This 'land' has the most teen appeal.

AMERICAN JOURNEYS

A brilliant CircleVision 360-degree presentation (see pages 38–9).

SPACE MOUNTAIN

The star ride in all Walt Disney World. The building housing this spectacular rollercoaster in the dark covers a staggering 10 acres and rises to a height of 180 feet. You may queue for quite a while – is it worth it? Just listen to all the screams to gauge the thrill content of a ride that lasts just about three minutes, seems to take forever and is definitely not for the fainthearted.

OTHER ATTRACTIONS

If you have small children in tow, take time off from queueing for the major set-piece rides described above and see Disneymania – live singing and dancing shows next to Cinderella's Castle, or Mickey's Starland, where Disney characters are always present for a cuddle and a photo-opportunity.

FANTASY IN THE SKY

For a magical end to what has probably been a magical day stick around to see the Magic Kingdom's firework display,

Hi ho! Dopey was never this tall in the movies!

Fantasy in the Sky. The lights go down, there is a hush and a spotlight plays on the top of Cinderella's Castle. Tinkerbell suddenly appears in a shower of magical pixie dust – you've seen it a hundred times before on TV but this is 'for real' – and floats down over the crowds (on a near-invisible guy-rope). The fireworks start, illuminating the castle, while a thousand cameras click and whirr.

Epcot

*E*pcot is an acronym for 'Experimental Prototype Community of Tomorrow' and (according to Disney) its flower-shaped logo symbolises 'Unity, fellowship, and harmony around the world. The outer rings are a celebration of life, the heart of the logo is Earth embraced by a star, to symbolise the hope that with imagination, commitment and dedication we can create a better world'. If it was not all so earnest, the word 'pretentious' would spring to mind, but certainly the Disney organisation has made an enormous financial commitment in its relentless endeavours to turn Walt Disney's vision into something approaching reality, albeit of a fantasyland style.

Epcot divides into two separate 'worlds'; Future World 'showing off the latest US technologies and the imagination of free enterprise', and World Showcase where the best bits of 11 countries have been transposed to fantasy pavilions. There is a full range of both international gourmet restaurants and less formal eating places in Epcot. Each venue is appropriately themed to its location within the park. The shops follow the same format and, with nearly 70 of them, World Showcase is a veritable international shopping mall.

FUTURE WORLD

As the brochure says, 'Dynamic themes are the driving forces of Future World'. Major corporations such as General Motors, AT&T, MetLife, Exxon, Nestlé, Kodak and United Technologies have combined their sponsorship and expertise with the creative talents of Disney's own designers and engineers to create a series of attractions which explain the technological wonders of the modern world, and provide vivid pointers to the bright new age which technology may one day bring to us.

HORIZONS

This ride takes its passengers through a DNA model; to see a space shuttle launch, and to discover future lifestyles in space, under the sea and in the desert.

INNOVENTIONS

Epcot's newest pavilion is Innoventions, which showcases products for the near future. Here the emphasis is on what will happen in the next five to 10 years, rather than what may happen in the next 50 to 100 years. Visitors can get their first taste of superhighway communications, CD–ROM libraries, virtual reality adventures and all sorts of smart new gadgets soon to be launched on commercial markets.

INNOVENTIONS EAST

Here, visitors can learn about the intricacies and workings of the computer

FORWARD TO THE FUTURE

The vision of the future as originally portrayed by Epcot (it opened in 1982 and therefore many of its concepts were based on late 1970s ideas) is in part looking decidedly old fashioned. Future World is therefore constantly under review and at present many areas are undergoing renovation with attractions changing all the time.

The future has never looked so good as it does at Epcot

age, as well as discovering the energy options of the future.

INNOVENTIONS WEST
A state-of-the-art telecommunications' showcase explained courtesy of Exxon, with the aid of some dazzling technological wizardry. Portrait sketching by robots is just one of the fascinating examples and there is a special teachers' unit providing educational media and study guides.

JOURNEY INTO IMAGINATION
Honey I Shrunk the Theater is Disney's latest 3-D movie which, combined with moving seats and other spectacular effects gives the impression of shrinking the audience, rather than 'the kids'. Mind that bee on the way out!

THE LAND
Agricultural technologies of the future, nutrition facts and a dramatic account of man's relationship with the natural world, make this one of the most interesting of Epcot's presentations.

The Land Pavilion – beautifully landscaped

THE LIVING SEAS
The wonders of the deep are explored in this very popular pavilion through a visit to an incredible man-made coral reef.

EPCOT

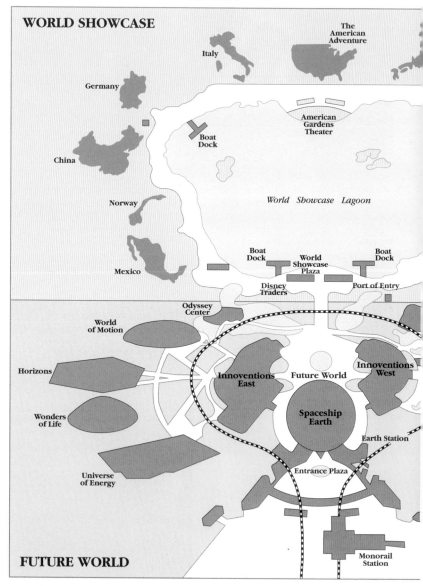

WORLD SHOWCASE

The American Adventure

Italy

Germany

American Gardens Theater

Boat Dock

China

World Showcase Lagoon

Norway

Boat Dock

Boat Dock

World Showcase Plaza

Mexico

Port of Entry

Disney Traders

Odyssey Center

World of Motion

Innoventions East

Future World

Innoventions West

Horizons

Spaceship Earth

Wonders of Life

Earth Station

Universe of Energy

Entrance Plaza

FUTURE WORLD

Monorail Station

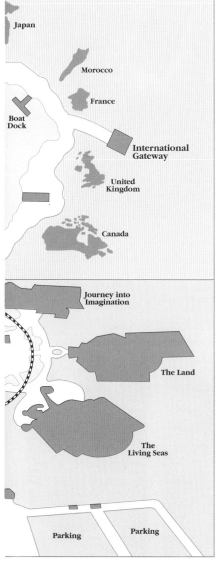

SPACESHIP EARTH

Nobody could fail to notice the massive golf ball-like structure at the entrance to Epcot. This ride spirals up the equivalent of 18 storeys within that shining sphere, revealing the dramatic history of communications and climaxing with a 'satellite view' from our own planet.

UNIVERSE OF ENERGY

A spectacular presentation which starts with a film on fossil fuels before the whole cinema ingeniously transforms itself into cars which trundle off into prehistory passing louring dinosaurs.

WONDERS OF LIFE

Body Wars provides a bumpy simulated journey through the human body on Epcot's most dramatic ride – good health and minimum size being conditions of climbing on board. There's a comical look at the workings of a 12-year-old's brain and a sensitive film presentation on the wonders of birth.

WORLD OF MOTION

General Motors explains what road transport is going to be like in the future and takes a light-hearted look at man's quest for mobility.

WORLD SHOWCASE

AMERICAN ADVENTURE

Almost every special visual and aural effect that has ever been devised (including a 72-foot wide rear projection screen and 35 of the most lifelike audio-animatronic models possible) is brought into play in this highly dramatised presentation of the struggles and triumphs of American history.

CANADA

Delightful floral beds, styled after Butchart Gardens in British Columbia, lead the visitor into the CircleVision 360-degree cinema (see pages 38–9). This literally surrounds the viewer with a dazzling showcase of Canada's great outdoor beauty.

CHINA

This pavilion hosts a spectacular CircleVision 360-degree film, along with a huge collection of valuable artefacts from the Orient.

FRANCE

The biggest attraction here, apart from the mini Eiffel Tower, is the atmospheric reproduction of France during its late 19th-century belle epoque, and (*bien sûr*) the food. There's also a 200-degree cinema film to enjoy.

GERMANY

There's no ride or cinema here but the fairy-tale architecture is impressive and if you enjoy the *bier garten* oompah atmosphere this is a good place to rest and drink awhile.

ITALY

Viewed from across the lagoon it looks for all the world like the real Venice. On the spot are strolling musicians, an Italian quartet and audience members press-ganged into playing roles in traditional folk tales.

JAPAN

Based on a replica of the venerable five-storey pagoda at Horyugi, the Japanese pavilion includes age-old art forms and the unmistakable soothing tones of Far Eastern music.

The best of British, Japanese and Moroccan architecture

Two enchanting corners of Europe: Italy (left), Germany (above)

comedy actors fracture Shakespeare with your help.

MEXICO

This atmospheric pavilion, set inside a huge pyramid, features a boat ride along the Rio del Tiempo (River of Time), a Mexican street market and a romantic *cantina* with strolling *mariachi* players.

MOROCCO

One of Epcot's most architecturally distinguished pavilions brings to life the atmosphere of the *souk* inside a walled desert city. Belly dancing is an attraction in the Marrakesh restaurant.

NORWAY

Take a ride on the *Maelstrom*, where treacherous trolls call up a savage North Sea storm.

UNITED KINGDOM

The popular Rose and Crown pub sets the Olde Worlde ambience while the traditional herb garden and maze are very pleasant refuges. A troupe of

WORLD SHOWCASE LAGOON

The World Showcase Lagoon is the stage for the fabulous rhapsody of music, fountains, lasers, lights and fireworks, known as Illuminations, which fills the air every evening.

THE GLOBAL SHOPPING VILLAGE

From among the many shops within Epcot, the following are some of the better buys: requisites for healthy living from Well & Goods Ltd (Wonders Of Life); Hummel and Goebel porcelain collectables (Germany); dolls, kimonos and Japanese handicrafts (Japan); fine wines, perfumes and Limoges china (France); Disney fashions and Kodak cameras (International Gateway); cashmere sweaters and tartan kilts (United Kingdom); Red Indian, Eskimo and Canadian arts and crafts (Canada).

Disney–MGM Studios

Unlike the Magic Kingdom and Epcot, the inspiration for Disney–MGM came not from within Walt Disney but from a competitor. Universal Studios, having enjoyed great success in California with their film theme park, announced their intention to open a major new film theme park in Orlando. Just in the nick of time Disney joined forces with MGM studios and in 1989 opened their park to steal a march on their rival.

In style the park is not unlike the Magic Kingdom. Main Street USA is replaced by Sunset Boulevard and Hollywood Boulevard, with appropriately themed shops, restaurants, street entertainers and modes of transport. Disney–MGM is the smallest of the three parks and you should be able to do it comfortably in a day. It is also the most adult-oriented of the parks and it helps to be a film buff, though even a passing acquaintance with the films that are featured will suffice.

RIDES AND ATTRACTIONS

ALADDIN'S ROYAL CARAVAN
Disney's hit cartoon-movie is brought to life with a parade of the film's favourite characters. A 32-foot-high genie leads the caravan, followed by acrobats, rope climbers, camels and snake charmers.

BACKSTAGE STUDIO TOUR
This fascinating insight as to how the movie and TV worlds function is conducted by tram and on foot. Highlights of the tour include a visit to the Creative Costuming Department; a walk through the 'streets' of New York and Roger Rabbit's Loony Bin props. In true cinematic style, there is a sting in the tail. The tour climaxes with a spectactular earthquake and flash-flood demonstrating modern disaster movie special effects.

During the tour you will see Disney–MGM is very much a working studio. You can see the areas where props and costumes are actually made and look inside actual film and TV studios.

BEAUTY AND THE BEAST
This Broadway-style production of Disney's Academy-Award winning classic is a favourite with all the family.

Gateway to the Stars – welcome to the movies

GREAT MOVIE RIDE

This disappointing ride is a homage to classic moments in the history of cinema, attempting to re-create such golden film memories as Gene Kelly *Singing In The Rain* and Bogart and Bergman's *Casablanca* farewell by the use of animatronics. Perhaps not surprisingly it doesn't work. Some things are better left to the memory or the silver screen. The monster from *Alien*, however, is quite scary and there's a cute finale from the *Wizard of Oz*. The frontage is a faithful replica of Hollywood's famed Graumann's Chinese Theater, complete with the stars' footprints.

DISNEY–MGM STUDIOS

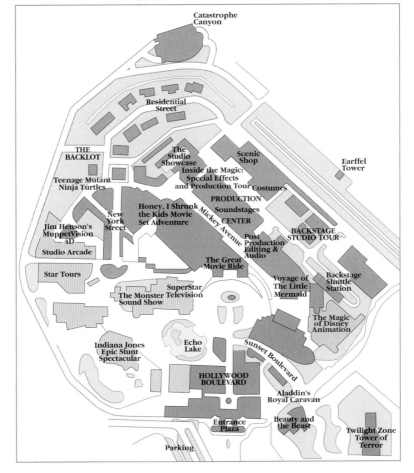

Look out for film stars and street entertainers on Hollywood Boulevard

HOLLYWOOD BOULEVARD
Art deco-style shops dominate the palm-tree lined roadway which leads from the main gate to the attractions.

HONEY, I SHRUNK THE KIDS
Climb on to the back of a giant bumble bee and discover what it feels like to be miniaturised. This clever adventure playground set, based on the popular film of the same name, is one for the kids.

RESTAURANTS AND DINERS
Of the many restaurants and catering outlets dotted throughout the park, the Hollywood Brown Derby Mama Melrose's Restaurant Italiano and the Sci-Fi Dine-in Theater Restaurant are specially recommended. In the latter, visitors sit in replicas of vintage convertibles while watching sci-fi clips and dining on junk food of a superior kind. The 1950s Prime Time Café evokes a convincing period atmosphere – a shame the prices don't do the same!

INDIANA JONES EPIC STUNT SPECTACULAR
A very popular large-scale outdoor stage presentation of some of the great adventurer's hairiest moments, using actors, film crew members and not a little audience participation.

INSIDE THE MAGIC: SPECIAL EFFECTS AND PRODUCTION TOUR
This fascinating one-hour walking tour is complementary to the Backstage Studio Tour and can be combined with it or taken separately. First up, you'll learn the secrets of how to shoot a naval battle on a peaceful-looking water tank, with the use of miniature boats, isolated camera shots and lots of splashing about. You can even don a sou'wester and yellow jacket and stand in the centre of the watery action if you wish!

More miniature props are employed to show how *Honey, I Shrunk the Kids* worked so effectively, and two lucky kids get to ride aboard a giant bumble bee on an actual film set.

An amusing Bette Midler short film,

The Lottery, shows the star climbing out on to balconies and generally having a hair-raising time in pursuit of a pigeon who has stolen her winning lottery ticket. Each scene is then replayed and taken apart, from the cameraman's angle, and you can see that things are very definitely not what they seem!

Finally, it's on to the post-production area to learn about sound tracks and then into the Disney cinema for a sneak preview of forthcoming attractions.

JIM HENSON'S MUPPETS ON LOCATION
Miss Piggy, Kermit, Gonzo and the rest of the gang star in a jokey musical showcase. This is probably for Muppet fans only.

JIM HENSON'S MUPPET VISION 3-D
A fun-packed three-dimensional movie, full of all the usual Muppet capers, plus state-of-the-art special effects. Not only do objects 'fly' out of the screen, the walls are alive too! Terrific fun whether you're a Muppet fan or not.

MAGIC OF DISNEY ANIMATION
Take yourself on a fascinating and educational self-guided tour through a real animation studio where you can watch Disney artists actually at work on future productions. Before that, see the Robin Williams-narrated film *Back To Neverland* for a rib-tickling look at the animation process. Finish with a tear-jerking trip back to your childhood courtesy of the classic cartoon re-runs in the Disney Classics Theatre.

SORCERY IN THE SKY
When the park has late opening hours do stay until the end of the day to see the night sky light up with a fabulous firework display (daily through the summer months, during holidays and special events). These are some of Disney's finest pyrotechnics, featuring a giant Mickey Mouse balloon, depicting the mouse as the Sorcerer's Apprentice (from *Fantasia*), which seems to orchestrate proceedings from high above Graumann's Chinese Theater.

Another close shave for Indy!

Graumann's Chinese Theater, home to the Great Movie Ride

SOUNDWORKS

An entertaining show where members of the audience create their own sound effects, bringing a special personal touch to classic movies, before graduating into the magic three-dimensional world of Soundsations. There's also the chance to add some spooky sound effects to the Chevy Chase/Martin Short movie, *Monster Sound*.

MGM SHOPPING

At Cover Story you can buy a mock magazine cover bearing your own mug shot and Oscar's Classic Car Souvenirs is packed with toys and models. Disney character-produce abounds, especially in Mickey's of Hollywood.

STAR TOURS

Before Universal Studios introduced their fabulous Back to the Future ride, this Star Fighter simulator ride, based on the film *Star Wars*, was acknowledged as the world's most exciting theme park simulator experience. It's still a stupendous ride, tearing off into outerspace through the meteor storms, then through the futuristic canyons of the Death Star. Star Tours is sponsored by M&M's chocolate candies, but don't eat them just before you climb aboard!

SUPERSTAR TELEVISION

Audience participation plays an important role here, with volunteers given the chance to co-star in classic excerpts from *I Love Lucy*, *Cheers*, *The*

Tonight Show and other TV hits. Even if you don't know the shows, don't be put off, it's very good fun – and quite educational too.

THE TWILIGHT ZONE TOWER OF TERROR

This is Walt Disney World's latest white-knuckle experience, unnerving in every respect as guests are invited to join the Twilight Zone. Riders start their adventure in the derelict 199-foot tall Hollywood Tower hotel. They then make their way through a mazey series of rooms with frightening special effects, culminating in a heart-stopping 13-storey plunge aboard a lift that is very definitely 'going down'.

Crossroads of the World, Hollywood Boulevard

Kowabunga! Meet the Turtles

VOYAGE OF THE LITTLE MERMAID

Puppets, lasers, live performers and clever special effects tell the Little Mermaid's story. Undoubtedly clever, if a bit tame.

THE MOUSE THAT ROARED

Smurfs and Muppets and Ninja Turtles may come and go but Mickey Mouse goes on for ever. Created in the midst of the 1930s Depression, this lovable character – now qualifying for an old age pension – has never lost his appeal for young and old alike.

Originally he was not going to be called Mickey (the name Mortimer was mooted) and his birth was in doubt, for the hopes of Walt Disney (his creator) had originally been pinned on another character called Oswald Rabbit. When the rabbit started to make a commercial impact, the young artist thought he was on his way, but a trip to New York produced a rude awakening. Somehow, he had let an unscrupulous distributor cheat him out of the rights to his creation. It was on the long train ride back home to Hollywood – as the locomotive clicketty-clacked across the endless plains of the Mid West – that Disney's idle doodling slowly evolved into the form of a perky little mouse.

Almost inadvertently, Disney had struck the right chord. With his eternal smile and upturned thumb, Mickey Mouse personified an enthusiasm and zest for life which was lacking in that grim era of economic collapse. And the never-resting pens and brushes of the master had soon created other lovable

characters to fill out the storylines of the animated cartoon movies which were to bring a much-needed smile to faces around the world.

Minnie Mouse, Donald Duck, Goofy, Pluto and many more joined the

growing pantheon of Disney stars and, with *Snow White*, his burgeoning studio produced a full-length cartoon feature which became one of childhood's best-loved fairy stories.

Better-known worldwide than even Father Christmas, Mickey Mouse symbolises what being young at heart is all about – which explains why so many adults, let alone children, are happy to dress in T-shirts bearing his ever-cheery face.

THE REST OF WALT DISNEY WORLD

If you take in all the attractions within Walt Disney World's three major theme parks you will have enough to fill every minute of an all-action one-week holiday. Yet, amazingly, Disney has even more on offer – and the expansion programme is never ending.

DISCOVERY ISLAND

Part of the Fort Wilderness complex (see below), this 11-acre zoological park, featuring exotic birds and animals, colourful flowers and peaceful trails, is reached by bridges across the channel in Bay Lake. Palms, bamboos and other tropical plants are viewed from meandering paths while Avian Way is one of the world's largest walk-through aviaries, featuring a breeding colony of scarlet ibis, along with white peacocks

and performing parrots. There are exotic land animals here too, including giant Galapagos tortoises.

Open: daily, in winter 10am–6pm; summer 10am–7pm. Admission charge.

DISNEY VILLAGE MARKETPLACE

The sheltered shores of Buena Vista Lagoon provide a very pleasant backdrop for leisurely shopping so why not do it here rather than wasting valuable theme-park 'ride-time'! The kids, meanwhile, can enjoy themselves on the lake's water sprites (see pages 132–3).

FORT WILDERNESS

Set amid stately pine and cypress trees, this pleasant and spacious campground is the centrepiece for 8,200 acres of nature trails and unspoilt wilderness. If you like meeting other families, it's a great place to spend a relaxing holiday and to be part of a loose-knit community. There are nearly 2,000 individual sites for both tents and caravans while some 400 comfortable and fully equipped trailers (static caravans) are available for rental, making a neat alternative form of budget accommodation within direct striking distance of all Walt Disney World's many attractions.

There are various sports facilities; basketball, volleyball, tennis, exercising and jogging are all catered for, while bicycles, tandems and canoes are available for hire.

Evening entertainment at the site includes a campfire singalong programme and marshmallow-toasting parties. If you want to attend the enormously popular Hoop-De-Doo Revue (accompanied by a rib-sticking barbecue-style meal), reservations should be made well in advance, by writing to

Discover Disney's own little paradise island

or calling Walt Disney World Reservations, PO Box 10,100, Lake Buena Vista FL 32830–0100. Tel: (407) 934–7639.

PLEASURE ISLAND

Disney's own nightlife complex is designed for a grown-up audience but accompanied children are admitted to most of the clubs as well as to the cinema (see page 138).

RIVER COUNTRY

Located within Fort Wilderness, this charming water park provides flumes, white-water rapids, water slides, a heated swimming pool, and a nature trail. Though considerably smaller than Disney's other water park (the spectacular Typhoon Lagoon) this extremely popular attraction has its own very special character, especially for those nostalgic for the kind of childhood where life revolved around a 'swimming hole' (the park's inspiration came from the stories of Huckleberry Finn and Tom Sawyer by Mark Twain). Rope-swings, a ship's boom and plenty of other aids to diving, jumping and generally making a big splash are all provided. Corkscrew

flumes set a faster pace to things. If you aren't keen on crowds, leave your visit until late afternoon and end the day by cooling down after traipsing round the theme parks.

Open: daily 10am–5pm; summer 10am–7pm (closed part of winter for renovation). Admission charge.

The attractions here are purely natural

TYPHOON LAGOON

Typhoon Lagoon is four times the size of Disney's River Country, which in its time was the trend-setting pioneer for all Orlando's water parks. Eight slippery slides and whitewater tubing flumes cascade from a 95-foot high watershed toward a lagoon where artificially created six-foot breakers send the surf rolling in to the shoreline of Central Florida. Most enervating of all is Humunga Kowabunga, two 214-foot long waterslides which take you down the slopes of Mount Mayday and through a series of caves at ever more breakneck speeds (if you lay back you will go even faster!).

Castaway Creek, a meandering 2,200-foot rafting stream encircles the 56-acre complex; it takes 25 minutes to complete a single leisurely circuit. Other favourites include the special Ketchakiddie Creek play area for children and the 362,000 gallon saltwater Shark Reef, where snorkellers can swim alongside colourful angel fish, rays and other reef creatures, including the fearsome looking but completely harmless nurse sharks.

Those who are less active can sit and soak up the sun in the park's lush tropical gardens.

Open: daily 10am–5pm (extended times in summer). Closed part of winter for renovation. Tel: (407) 824–4321 for schedules. Admission charge.

Wet 'n' Wild is as thrilling or as relaxing as you care to make it

WET, WET, WET!

When it's time to cool off, there's no need to head for the coast. Besides, Disney's water holes (see pages 85–6) Orlando boasts two other thrilling aquaparks. Wet 'n' Wild on International Drive has long been known as the biggest and most exciting in the area, but Kissimmee's Water Mania has recently been revamped and also has a faithful following.

WATER MANIA

Water Mania hasn't as many exhilarating rides as Wet 'n' Wild but it boasts two of the best in town, with the award-winning Wipe Out, a simulated body-surfing ride, and the Abyss, a tube slide through 300 feet of darkness. If you want more try the 72-foot Screamer or the tortuous Anaconda. There's family rides too and a 'pirate ship' for water babies.
West Irlo Bronson Memorial Highway (US 192), Kissimmee. Open: daily except 1 to 25 December. Tel: (407) 396–2626 for schedule.

WET 'N' WILD

Renowned for the quantity and quality of its watery thrills, Wet 'n' Wild never rests on its laurels and continues to introduce bigger and scarier rides. The park's latest blockbuster is the Surge, Florida's biggest and longest multi-passenger water ride with more than 580 feet of curves, while Bubba Tub sends groups of up to five riders at a time twisting and turning through banked curves during a giddying drop from a six-storey high tower. There's also the unique new Bomb Bay, which features a bomb-shaped capsule dropped in virtual free-fall down a 76-foot high, 79-degree waterslide. Two more thrill slides not to be missed are Der Stuka (not for those with vertigo) and The Black Hole (a sort of Cresta Run in the dark). It's not all heart-in-the-mouth stuff however. You can ride Mammoth River or try a variety of slides, chutes, flumes and pools until you find one that suits your level.
6200 International Drive, Orlando. Open: times vary throughout the year. Tel: (407) 351–3200 for a schedule.

Beyond Orlando

*W*hen the hustle and bustle of International Drive starts to wear thin, take a drive out to the delightful west of Orlando. Here, horse ranches, citrus farms and personal museum collections offer a less frenetic form of entertainment.

APPLETON MUSEUM OF ART

Amassed by industrialist and horse breeder Arthur I Appleton, this superb collection of fine art spans 5,000 years of civilisation around the world through more than 6,000 artefacts (4,000 of which are on display at any one time). Pre-Columbian South American art, Chinese coral and jade carvings, Etruscan pottery, African wood carvings and masks, European glassware and guns are just some of the beautifully displayed pieces on view here.
Location: 75 miles NW of Orlando. 4333 East Silver Springs Boulevard, Ocala. Tel: (904) 236–5056. Open: Tuesday to Saturday 10am–4.30pm; Sunday 1am–5pm. Admission charge.

Tricoteuse by William Adolphe Bougereau – Appleton Museum of Art

CENTRAL FLORIDA RAILROAD MUSEUM

A train spotter's heaven with a mind-boggling collection of railway artefacts which are housed in the old Tavares and Gulf Railway depot in Winter Garden's suburbs.
Location: Winter Garden. Tel: (407) 656–8749. Opening times vary (phone for schedules). Admission charge.

DON GARLITS' MUSEUM OF DRAG RACING

This is the world's only museum dedicated to those spectacular machines that tear along a ¼-mile straight in under seven seconds. There are over 60 drag-racing cars dating from the earliest 1940s models and, for cognoscenti of the sport, these include cars belonging to Tom McEwen, Shirley Muldowney, Art Malone and of course 'Big Daddy' Don Garlits. Another 40 or so antique cars are also on display, including one of the finest collections of early Fords to be found anywhere.
Location: 15 miles south of Ocala. 13700 South West 16th Avenue, Ocala. Tel: (904) 245–8661. Open: daily 9am–5.30pm. Admission charge.

FLORIDA CITRUS TOWER

This towering 226-foot high landmark is Florida's highest observation point, at 546 feet above sea level. It was built

Ranch at Ocala

purely as a tourist attraction in order that visitors to the Sunshine State could enjoy the sight of the citrus groves stretching out over the rolling hills below. Unfortunately in recent years this has been something of an anti-climax due to extensive frost damage.

In the area at the foot of the tower you can see some of the fruit processing methods and board a tram for a tour of the groves.

Location: US 27 North. Clermont is 24 miles west of Orlando. Tel: (904) 394–8585. Open: daily 8am–6pm. Admission charge.

MOUNT DORA

If you like antiques, this unspoiled little village is for you. Set on the shores of Lake Dora, the faithfully restored historic downtown area has shops crammed with bric-à-brac. Mount Dora is also renowned for its wedding cake architecture, with numerous classic examples of Victorian Gothic, including

---

LIVESTOCK FARMS

Horse breeding is big business in the Ocala area and a number of Florida Thoroughbred Breeders' Association members around here are happy to show visitors around their premises. It is essential to book an appointment in advance by phone.

Monday: Good Chance Farm. Tel: (904) 245–1136. Tuesday: Florida Stallion Station. Tel: (904) 629–4416. Wednesday: Bridlewood Farm. Tel: (904) 622–5319. Thursday: Live Oak Stud. Tel: (904) 854–2691. Friday: Ocala Stud Farm. Tel: (904) 237–2171. Saturday and Sunday: Ocala Breeders' Sales Company and Training Center. Tel: (904) 237–2154. Early morning workouts take place between 7am–9am.

---

the Donelly House, which looks like a grounded steamboat. Antique swords are exhibited in the old fire station's Royellou Museum (between 4th and 5th Avenues, off Baker Street).

Location: 45 miles northwest of Orlando.

Backwoods and Springs

*T*he heart of unspoiled north and west central Florida offers plenty of opportunities to see natural Florida at its best. Kids don't always see the fun of getting away from it all however, which is where 'natural theme parks' such as Silver Springs and Weeki Wachee come in handy.

HOMOSASSA SPRINGS STATE PARK

This beautiful natural park is probably the best place in all Florida to see manatees (see pages 92–3). Once in the park you are taken to the wonderfully named Spring of Ten Thousand Fish by boat. You then board a floating observatory which allows you to go below the surface of the spring to see the manatees, together with a multitude of fresh- and salt-water fish. Displays along the park's nature trails include an extensive collection of wild birds.
Location: 24 miles north of Weeki Wachee Spring (112 miles) northwest of Orlando. 9225 W Fishbowl Drive, Homosassa. Tel: (904) 628–5343. Open: daily 9am–5.30pm. Admission charge.

OCALA NATIONAL FOREST

It's easy to find peace and solitude here among the world's largest sand pine forest. The favourite spot for most visitors, however, is the Juniper Springs State Recreation Area. There is a visitor centre housed in a picturesque old mill house where a huge wheel rolls over 8 million US gallons of spring water every day. And you can get right into the water on a 7-mile canoe trip, paddling peacefully downstream enjoying the flora and fauna. Wet 'n' Wild it ain't, but it might just be the highlight of your holiday.
Location: Juniper Springs Recreation Area is on US 40, 36 miles east of Ocala. Tel:

(904) 625–2520. Open: daily dawn to dusk. Free.

SILVER SPRINGS

At the heart of this natural wonderland is the largest artesian limestone spring in the world, pumping 750 million US gallons each day. The highlights of a visit here are the three boat trips which take you through crystal-clear waters into a primeval and exotic Floridian landscape. Water birds, alligators and turtles are here in abundance. Aboard the Jungle Cruise trip you'll also see monkeys (a legacy of six of the original *Tarzan* movies that were filmed here), giraffes, gazelles, emus and other introduced wildlife, all roaming freely, constrained only by the natural island landscapes.

In addition to the boat rides there's a jeep safari, an excellent reptile show, a petting zoo and Dinosaurs Alive, a clever audio-animatronic world of prehistoric monsters (additional charge). Wild Waters, the adjacent water park (additional charge, open summer only) completes a full day out here.
Location: 75 miles northwest of Orlando. 5656 NE Florida Boulevard (SR 40). Tel: (904) 236–2121. Open: daily 9am–5pm (later in summer). Admission charge.

WEECHI WACHEE SPRINGS

Wacky is just about the right word for this attraction which combines natural Florida at its most beautiful with a theme-show that is Florida at its most kitsch. Based next to the large natural spring, the centrepiece of the park is a mermaid show in a huge glass tank. The performers are 'dancing girls', complete with tails, who sustain their bizarre yet impressive underwater theatrical performance by taking lungfuls of air from submerged air lines.

To restore your sanity, take the Wilderness River Cruise which sails along one of the beautiful rivers off the spring and look out for creatures of a more plausible kind – raccoons, alligators and so on. There's also a Birds of Prey show, a petting zoo and a small water park fed by the spring, known as Buccaneer Bay, where kids can splash to their heart's content.

Location: US 19/Route 50 intersection. 88 miles west of Orlando. Tel: (904) 596–2062. Open: daily 9.30am–5.30pm. Admission charge.

Silver Springs – Jeep Safari (below) and Jungle Cruise (bottom)

MANATEES

The manatee comes from the mammalian order *sirenia* and is a type of sea cow, distantly related to the elephant, found in the tropical coastal waters of America, the West Indies and Africa. It is a huge lumbering amorphous barrel of an animal, weighing up to 3,500 pounds, perpetually wrinkled, with a whiskery face, thick grey-brown skin and tiny eyes.

In summer, manatees have been known to range as far afield as Texas to the west and Virginia and the Carolinas to the north. But in winter, herds are concentrated in Florida, where six natural springs and 19 clean, warm-water, power-plant discharge areas maintain water temperatures close to 72°F.

They are so slow, so gentle and docile, that they easily evoke affection and have no natural predators. Yet they are disappearing fast. Not many years ago, manatees were common in Florida's waters. Now there are estimated to be just 2,000 left. Scientists have predicted that within a decade they may be extinct.

Man's relationship with the manatee

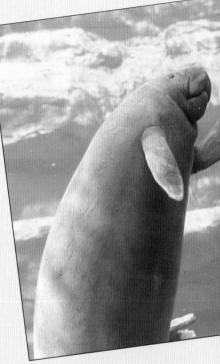

goes back to antiquity. Ancient mythology spoke of creatures that were half-fish, half woman and it is possible that the mermaid legend may be based upon the manatee, or at least the sea cow family. Columbus recorded a manatee sighting during 1493, though he noted that as mermaid mythology went, this was rather an ugly specimen!

Indians and early settlers hunted the manatees for food and Cowpens Key in Florida is believed to have taken its name from the watery corrals where manatees were herded. Their thick hides were used for leather, their blubber oil for cooking and lighting, and their ivory-like bones for carving. Yet

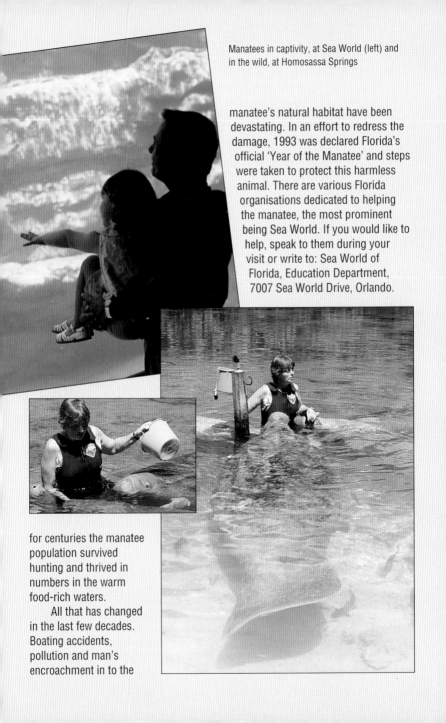

Manatees in captivity, at Sea World (left) and in the wild, at Homosassa Springs

manatee's natural habitat have been devastating. In an effort to redress the damage, 1993 was declared Florida's official 'Year of the Manatee' and steps were taken to protect this harmless animal. There are various Florida organisations dedicated to helping the manatee, the most prominent being Sea World. If you would like to help, speak to them during your visit or write to: Sea World of Florida, Education Department, 7007 Sea World Drive, Orlando.

for centuries the manatee population survived hunting and thrived in numbers in the warm food-rich waters.

All that has changed in the last few decades. Boating accidents, pollution and man's encroachment in to the

Winter Park

Founded as a rich man's winter retreat from the rigours of New York and other northern cities, the trim, well-manicured little town of Winter Park is filled with shady trees and colourful flowers plus fashionable boutiques, popular street cafés and fine restaurants. *You could cover this walk in an hour or so but allow at least half a day.*

Start from the Albin Polasek Studio on Osceola Avenue, before entering Rollins College campus.

1 CORNELL FINE ARTS MUSEUM

The superb museum of American and European art here is said to be the biggest of its kind in Central Florida and its collection is rotated on a six-weekly basis to give everything a showing. The Cornell Galleries host regular classical concerts while the nearby Annie Russell Theater is renowned for its summer repertory series.

2 ROLLINS COLLEGE

The fine Spanish Colonial/Italianate architecture of this venerable institution is best viewed from the placid waters of Lake Virginia (see Scenic Boat Rides, below). It is Florida's oldest college (founded 1885) and remains one of the most select schools in America.
Join Park Avenue at its southernmost end and walk north.

3 PARK AVENUE

Art galleries, trendy restaurants and shops filled with expensive ornaments and *haute couture* proliferate along Winter Park's main street. City Hall is small but worth a look and close by is the renowned Park Plaza Hotel. If you are in Winter Park on a Saturday morning take a detour down New England Avenue to visit the colourful Farmers' Market (see page 135).

Cornell Fine Arts Museum
Tel: (407) 646–2526. Open: Tuesday
to Friday 10am–5pm, Saturday and
Sunday 1–5pm. Free.
Morse Museum of American Art
Tel: (407) 645–5311. Open: Tuesday
to Saturday 9.30am–4pm, Sunday
1–4pm. Admission charge.
Scenic Boat Tours
Tel: (407) 644–4056. Tours run daily
10am–4.30pm.

Rollins College campus

4 CENTRAL PARK

Amtrak railway, which links Miami with
the north, runs parallel with Park Avenue
along the opposite side of the park. The
trains, with their evocative horns, run
four times a day and are a majestic sight
as they trundle slowly by. Look for the
fine fountain statue, *Emily,* by Albin
Polasek.
*Detour right into East Welbourne Avenue
and walk along it for a few yards.*

Tiffany lamps from the superb collection in
the Morse Gallery of Art

5 MORSE GALLERY OF ART

Charles Hosmer Morse, who bestowed
Central Park on Winter Park, is
remembered in the name of this lovely
gallery on East Welbourne Avenue. It is
world famous for its magnificent collection
of Tiffany glass, most of it rescued from
the demolished Laurelton Hall, Long
Island, once the home of Louis Comfort
Tiffany (1848–1933). Lalique glassware
also features prominently, alongside
jewellery and ornaments.
*Return to Park Avenue and continue
northwards to East Morse Boulevard. Turn
right and walk down to the lakeside.*

6 SCENIC BOAT TOURS

Thanks to connecting canals, dug to
facilitate the logging trade, one-hour
boat trips visit the three lakes of Osceola,
Maitland and Virginia.
*Retrace your steps and turn right on to Park
Avenue. Brandywine Square is on the
opposite side of the road, a block north.*

7 BRANDYWINE SQUARE

A nice spot to stop for a coffee and some
cake. There are arts and crafts shops too
in this neatly renovated quarter.
*Return down the opposite pavement of Park
Avenue to rejoin Osceola Avenue.*

North of Orlando

Just north of metropolitan Orlando lies a land of sleepy country towns, expansive citrus groves, woodlands and water. There aren't any high-speed thrills or theme parks on this tour, but there is still something for all the family. *Allow a day.*

Take I–4 north to exit 51. From here SR 46 East takes you to downtown Sanford.

1 SANFORD

This pleasant market town lies at the heart of a thriving agricultural community and makes the extravagant claim of being 'the celery capital of the world'. Of rather more interest to curious visitors are its carefully preserved Victorian buildings and its site on Lake Monroe. The lake is one of many into which the St John's river flows and Sanford commands the final navigable section of this once-important waterway.

Authoress Harriet Beecher Stowe made her home on the banks of the river and perhaps took inspiration from here for *Uncle Tom's Cabin*. After she had become famous, canny riverboat companies payed the distinguished lady to wave to their passengers from her riverside lawn. The commercial transportation services have long gone but you can still enjoy the gracious age of the St John's on a leisurely riverboat cruise (see pages 122–3).
Head five miles west on US17–92.

2 CENTRAL FLORIDA ZOO

A small but important collection of around 250 birds and animals, including primates, hippos, otters and members of the cat family. A petting centre and elephant and pony rides (weekends only) keep young ones amused.
Cross the St John's River on US 17–92 and continue through Orange City. Turn left on

West French Avenue and head west for two miles.

3 BLUE SPRINGS STATE PARK

A favoured winter home for Florida's famous manatees (see pages 92–3), who enjoy the constant 72°F waters. An alternative viewing point can be obtained by detouring to the peace of nearby Hontoon River Landing (see pages 122–3).

Retrace your journey to US 17–92. Turn left and continue for two miles. Turn right on SR 472 then left on to Cassadaga Road. Just after it crosses I–4, follow the signs to Cassadaga.

4 CASSADAGA

Spiritualism is the business which keeps this eccentric little community going. Whether you take it seriously, or treat it as a bit of fun, the delightfully named Purple Rose Metaphysical Stuff Store makes an interesting stop-off.

Return to I–4 and head north to the junction with the SR 44 to De Land.

5 DE LAND

Once a cattle centre, De Land is now home to the handsome porticoed Stetson University. Main Street contrasts the thoroughly modern Cultural Arts Center and DeLand Museum of Art with distinguished DeLand Hall, which is the oldest building in Florida in continuous

New York Avenue, De Land

use for higher education (established 1884). Henry Addison DeLand House holds artefacts which once belonged to the city's founder.

Take US 17–92 north for 9 miles (taking the left fork on US 17 when US 92 breaks off to the east).

6 DE LEÓN SPRINGS

Good swimming and canoeing are to be had in this important natural spring which pumps 19-million US gallons into the St John's River each day. A highlight of the park is the Old Spanish Sugar Mill, now a restaurant.

Return to Orlando on US 17–92.

Beautiful unspoilt De León Springs

Central Florida Zoo
Tel: (407) 323–4450. Open: daily
9am–5pm.
Cultural Arts Center and DeLand Museum of Art
Tel: (904) 734–4371. Open: Tuesday to Saturday 10am–4pm, Sunday 1–4pm.

St Augustine

A strong contender for the title of America's oldest city, the attractive colonial settlement of St Augustine was established in 1565 by Pedro Menéndez de Avilés, 55 years before the Pilgrim Fathers reached New England. Happily it has managed to preserve much of its proud past and still boasts many buildings which were built when the Spaniards were the colonial masters of Florida. Moreover, it's almost purpose-built for walkers, with its narrow and often pedestrianised streets. *Allow a full day.*

Start at the old City Gate, where San Marco Avenue becomes Avenida Menéndez.

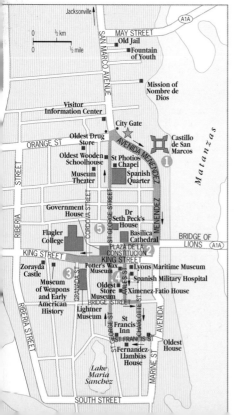

1 CASTILLO DE SAN MARCOS

Strategically placed to cover the broad Matanzas river and access to the sea, the present fortress was begun in 1672 and took 25 years to complete. The ornate gateway, made from a mix of cement and seashells, replaced the earlier wooden entrance burnt by the attacking British in 1702. There's a commanding view and photo opportunities galore from the impressive ramparts with their distinctive domed sentry boxes.
Take a horse and carriage ride or walk south along Avenida Menéndez towards the Bridge of Lions.

2 PLAZA DE LA CONSTITUCIÓN

This picturesque colonial square is very Spanish in character and appearance, flanked by Government House and the Basilica Cathedral of St Augustine.
Cross to the south side and turn right on King Street.

3 LIGHTNER MUSEUM

The former Alcazar Hotel, built in splendid Spanish-Colonial style in 1888, now houses a formidable collection of furnishings, antiques, musical instruments, Tiffany glass and much more. The displays were amassed by newspaper baron Otto C Lightner and gifted to the town in 1948. Across the street is Flagler College, an important educational institution housed in a contemporary and similarly styled old hotel. An elegant courtyard leads to the ornate foyer with its carved oak, imported marble and Tiffany glass. Tours of the building are conducted. *Retrace your steps to Avilés Street.*

4 HISTORIC ST AUGUSTINE

Packed into the compact centre of old St Augustine is a dazzling selection of venerable houses, some eclectic museums and historical attractions, including the reconstructed Spanish Military Hospital, the Oldest Store Museum and the town's oldest inn, the St Francis, which opened in 1791. The González-Alvares House at 14 Francis Street, is the town's much visited 'Oldest House', but the entire area evokes memories of colonial times, with ornate architecture, overhanging balconies and a profusion of gardens and flowers.

OPENING TIMES

All the attractions featured in this walk open Monday to Saturday 9am–5pm (or later) and on Sunday from noon–5pm. Many open Sunday morning as well. All charge for admission. For more details call the St Augustine Visitor Center, tel: (904) 829–5681. As an overnight stay is recommended (it's a 98-mile journey from Orlando on often slow roads), enquire about accommodation, particularly in some of the town's attractive and historic inns.

This excellent museum was once a palatial railway hotel

5 ST GEORGE STREET

This is the charming pedestrianised hub of the tourist district, with pretty streets criss-crossing it. Built before 1750, Dr Seth Peck's House was, in turn, the Spanish settlers' treasury and home to the British governor. Craftworkers in period Spanish dress can usually be watched at work in the Spanish Quarter complex, with its 250-year old houses set in delightful gardens. Adjacent, the St Photios Chapel is revered as a national shrine by Greek immigrants to the US; the first of them settled near Daytona, in 1768 and moved to St Augustine nine years later. Also worth visiting nearby are the Oldest Wooden Schoolhouse and the Oldest Drug Store.
Continue along St George Street to get back to the City Gate.

NASA Kennedy Space Center, Spaceport USA

Spaceport USA is a mecca for anyone who's ever wondered what it's like to be an astronaut or who simply enjoys gazing at space rockets. Don't worry if you find the technical detail of some of the displays daunting, skim these bits and enjoy the amazing large-scale films and the site tours.

It's an easy 56-mile journey from Orlando and with its welcome free-admission policy (a small charge is made for the films and the tours), Spaceport USA justifies its claim as Florida's best-value visitor attraction.

GUIDED TOURS
Guided coach tours of the Space Center run daily on a continual basis and go from the central exhibition area, known as the Galaxy Center. There are two tours available; both last around two hours, though you do get off the coach to see various exhibits.

Reach for the Sky! Historic space craft in the Rocket Park

If this is your first visit, opt for the Red Tour, which goes to the Apollo Mission and Space Shuttle sites. The Blue Tour goes to Cape Canaveral to see the pioneer space-flight bases. Stops are quite frequent (operations permitting) and the Red Tour will take you into a re-creation of the launch control room used for the first moon landing in 1969. You will then continue on, to gaze in awe at the 3,000 US-ton Giant Crawler Shuttle

Transporter. This is basically a giant platform (around half the size of a football pitch) on four gigantic caterpillar tracks which rumbles along at 1mph, transporting the Space Shuttle from the Vehicle Assembly Building (VAB) to the launch pad. Spaceport USA's newest exhibit is a full-scale space shuttle replica. The VAB is enormous too – in terms of capacity, one of the largest buildings in the world. This superlative tour culminates in a close look at the largest American space rocket ever built – Saturn V (the Apollo moon-mission power-pack) measuring 363 feet long and weighing some 31,000 US tons.

IMAX FILMS

Back at the Galaxy Center don't miss seeing at least one of the three IMAX films on show. IMAX is a special, very large-scale cinema technique: here projected on to a massive five-storey high screen. It draws you right into the picture as a simulator does. Don't miss *The Dream is Alive*. This tells the story of recent space exploration and when the Space Shuttle blasts off the feeling of power is awesome. Some of the footage was actually shot by the astronauts in space.

There are other films to enjoy in the complex and a wide range of hardware in the Gallery of Space Flight. The most impressive exhibits, however (aside from those on the tour) are the actual rockets in the 'rocket park', which greet you at the entrance to the Galaxy Center.

You will need five to six hours to do justice to all that's here, though a quicker tour is feasible. Finally take time to pause at the simple but moving Astronaut's Memorial. Despite all the high-tech wizardry that is on call here, space travel is still a highly dangerous business.

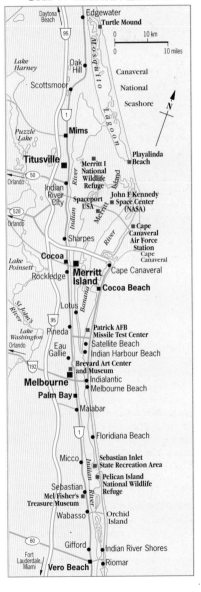

CAPE CANAVERAL

Astronaut Memorial Hall – a tribute to America's space pioneers

OTHER SPACE COAST ATTRACTIONS

ASTRONAUT MEMORIAL HALL

Visit the planetarium to explore the universe through Florida's largest telescope, then relive America's first days in space with the original seven astronauts, who have contributed their own personal experiences (including recorded voices, and treasured mementoes) to create this fascinating experience. Laser shows are given on Friday and Saturday nights.
Brevard College, 1519 Clearlake Road, Cocoa. Tel: (407) 242–0737. Open: daily 10am–4pm. Free. Admission charge for Planetarium.

BREVARD ART CENTER AND MUSEUM

This art lover's haven is internationally renowned for its visiting exhibitions from both contemporary artists and major collections. It is housed in a light and airy modern building which has itself won awards.
1463 North Highland Avenue, Melbourne. Tel: (407) 242–0737. Open: Tuesday to Saturday 10am–4pm. Admission charge.

UNITED STATES ASTRONAUT HALL OF FAME

This is a showcase for America's astronauts and their historic missions. Bang up to date, however, is a full-scale replica of the space shuttle orbiter where visitors take a 12-minute space trip through a multi-sensory video show.
NASA Parkway (SR405), Titusville. Tel: (407) 269–6100. Open: daily 8am–dusk. Admission charge.

VALIANT AIR COMMAND MUSEUM

More than 350 warbirds, dating back to World War II are on display. Founded in 1977, the museum keeps these superb old planes in pristine flying condition.

Space Center Executive Airport, 6600 Tico Road, Titusville. Tel: (407) 268–1941.

NATURE ON THE SPACE COAST

Co-existing with science at its most futuristic, the barrier islands, marshlands, beaches and creeks of the Space Coast represent a jealously guarded preserve for all manner of wildlife.

MERRITT ISLAND NATIONAL WILDLIFE REFUGE

This nature conservation area covers 220 square miles of wetlands and is home to 310 species of birds, 117 fish species and 25 different mammals. Great blue herons, wood storks and egrets are common and a car trail and footpaths make it all quite accessible. A pleasant visitor centre has displays of what to see.

Titusville. Tel: (407) 867–0667. Visitor Center open: Monday to Friday 8am–4.30pm, Saturday and Sunday 9am–7pm. Free.

PLAYALINDA BEACH

This is one of Florida's least spoilt and most secluded stretches of seashore. Boardwalk crossings give access to the beach without endangering the native dune vegetation. Hundreds of giant sea

---

UNITED STATES SPACE CAMP FLORIDA

Youngsters from eight to 14 will find the Space Camp in Titusville an unforgettable experience, offering them the chance to use astronaut training simulators from the Mercury, Gemini and Apollo space programmes. This five-day 'hands-on' educational adventure includes building and launching model rockets, constructing a space station and even sampling a freeze-dried astronaut meal. Pre-registration is essential; tel: (toll-free within the US) 1–800–63–SPACE or (407) 269–6100).

US Space Camp is on the same site as the Astronaut Hall of Fame.

---

turtles come here each year to lay their eggs on the beach.

TURKEY CREEK SANCTUARY

A 4,000-foot boardwalk gives views of three distinct plant habitats and the birds and other creatures they support.

1502 Port Malabar Boulevard, Palm Bay. Tel: (407) 952–3400.

Valiant Air Command Museum

WINDOW ON THE UNIVERSE

In 1958 the National Aeronautics and Space Administration body (NASA) was set up at Cape Canaveral Air Force Station on Florida's wild northeast

coast. Just three years later NASA and the whole of America celebrated the success of the first American manned space mission. By 1964 the space race had reached new heights and the re-named NASA Kennedy Space Center was re-located the short distance to its present base on Merritt Island. Since then the Apollo missions have put man on the moon and have launched and re-launched several Space Shuttles.

The public's right to share in all of this was enshrined in the original laws which created NASA. These specifically identified the importance of public interest and charged NASA to share their successes (and failures) with the American people.

Visitors to the site are nothing new. As long ago as 1963, during the Mercury mission era, Cape Canaveral was opened to the public for three hours each Sunday. By the time Cape Kennedy opened just a year later, annual attendances were up to 400,000.

And by 1989 the number of annual visitors had topped three million.

To accommodate such numbers, a permanent 70-acre visitor facility was opened six miles inside Gate 3 on the main road in from Orlando. Now known as Kennedy Space Center Spaceport USA, the complex comprises seven separate exhibit areas, and bus tours of the site leave from here.

Updated information on forth-coming launches, which always draw

The launch of a Space Shuttle (below is *Discovery*) is always an awesome experience, but you have to apply long before the event

huge crowds, is available from NASA (tel: (407) 867–4636) or from Spaceport USA (tel: 1–800–SHUTTLE, in Florida only).

Prime viewing sites lie along US Highway 1, in the Titusville area, and along Highway A1A around the Atlantic beach conurbations of Cape Canaveral and Cocoa Beach.

Free tickets to watch the spectacle from a special viewing area, six miles from the launch site, can be obtained by writing (three months in advance) to NASA Visitor Services, Mail Code: PA-PASS, Kennedy Space Center, FL 32899. The same site can be reached by special buses departing from Spaceport USA. Reservations are required and tickets must be collected in person prior to launch day. Do beware, however, that launches are often delayed (sometimes for days on end) and while they are in progress there is restricted site access.

Cocoa Beach

As the closest seaside town to Orlando, Cocoa Beach naturally attracts lots of day visitors. It is also a popular resort in its own right, though it has a somewhat jaded look and would appear to have seen better days. Separated from the mainland by the marshes and placid salt waters of the broad Indian River and the Banana River, Cocoa Beach straggles along one of the islands which stretch down this coast. Mile upon mile of often tacky ribbon development along the oceanfront eventually gives way to vast unspoiled stretches of low sand dunes where you have the beach all to yourself. Beware, however, the Atlantic waters can be cold and rough. *Allow a full day.*

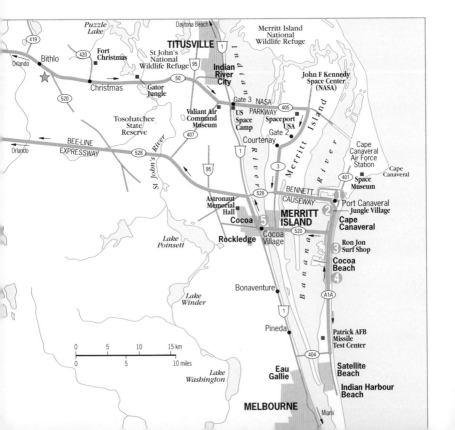

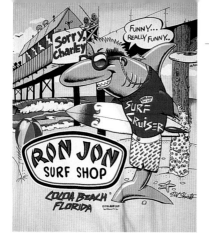

Leave Orlando on SR 50, travelling east. Pass through the tiny settlement of Christmas, remarkable for its Christmas tree, decorated all year round. After 17 miles you will pass Gator Jungle Indian Village where alligators and the rare Florida panther can be seen in their natural habitat. Cross to the islands via SR 528 and a series of causeways and bridges after passing the turn-off for the Kennedy Space Center.

1 PORT CANAVERAL

This is the Space Coast's most important commercial port. Port Canaveral is the main base for cruise ships serving the Caribbean and the Bahamas. There are mini-cruises to Nassau aboard the *Star Ship Oceanic*. Smaller vessels cruise the Florida Intracoastal Waterway.
Continue south on the A1A.

2 JUNGLE VILLAGE

A family fun centre with three go-kart tracks, two 18-hole mini-golf courses and one of the biggest amusement arcades on the Space Coast.
Continue south on the A1A.

3 RON JON SURF SHOP

This vast building contains everything the surfer needs.
Continue south on the A1A.

4 COCOA BEACH

A laid-back resort with no definable centre, being a straggle of hotels, motels, condominiums and private houses, which eventually peters out near Patrick Air Force Base. One block apart, two parallel roads, both designated A1A, cut through the southern section of Cocoa Beach, the one closest to the ocean taking the southbound traffic. When it comes to choosing a bit of beach, the stretch behind the Holiday Inn Hotel enables you to enjoy their facilities. Cocoa Beach Pier is extremely popular with anglers.
Retrace your route north along A1A to the SR 520 where you should turn left. After crossing the Banana River and the Indian River, look for Cocoa Village on the left.

5 COCOA VILLAGE

A taste of more leisurely times in an unpretentious, unspoiled little river port, with a potpourri of neat shops and places to relax.
Return to Orlando via the SR 520 and the SR 528 Bee-Line Expressway.

FORT CHRISTMAS
Tel: (407) 568–4149. Open: Tuesday to Saturday 10am–5pm, Sunday 1–5pm. Free.
GATOR JUNGLE INDIAN VILLAGE
Tel: (407) 568–2885. Open: daily 9am–6pm. Admission charge.
PORT CANAVERAL
Star Ship Oceanic (Premier Cruise Lines) – tel: (602) 207–1049. Capt JP Cruises, Mariner Square Marina, Cocoa – tel: (407) 635–8722.
JUNGLE VILLAGE
Tel: (407) 783–0595. Open: daily 10am–midnight.

Daytona Beach

The inspiration for the development of Daytona into one of America's best known seaside resorts was its 23-mile long broad sandy beach. These days it's a modern, cheap and cheerful sort of place but there is enough faded grandeur around to bring a strong whiff of nostalgia for childhood holidays spent in similar spots. Given the backdrop of high-rise hotels and apartments and firm, gently sloping sands, where the tide goes out a very long way, European visitors might liken the resort to the Belgian coast. However, here the sun shines relentlessly. *Allow 2 hours.*

Daytona Beach is reached from Orlando by driving northeast on Interstate 4 (allow 2 hours). You can park on the beach itself. Ocean Pier makes an ideal starting point.

1 OCEAN PIER

The end of this grand old structure – claimed to be the longest pier on the whole of America's east coast – provides a sweeping view of the famous beach. A favourite spot for anglers, the pier has other attractions, including the old casino, with its original ornate mirrors still in place. A gondola ride, short but fun, gives great views, as does the spiralling ride up the Pier's Space Needle. *Return to the Boardwalk and turn north.*

2 THE BOARDWALK

Faded postcards from the 1930s show the Boardwalk at its zenith. Many of the art deco style frontages remain. Amusement

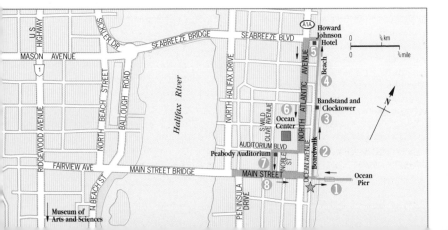

In the land of the automobile the car goes right to the water's edge – not even the beach is safe!

arcades and miniature golf can be found at the Boardwalk's park. Sundays bring hundreds of vendors and thousands of bargain hunters to a huge flea market.
Walk along the Boardwalk.

3 THE BANDSTAND AND CLOCK TOWER

Free weekly concerts and a range of other events are presented at the 1930s bandstand while the ornate Clock Tower was erected in 1935 as a tribute to Sir Malcolm Campbell's record-breaking run (see below).
Step off the Boardwalk on to the beach.

4 THE BEACH

The swimming is safe and the sand is perfect for making the most ornate of sandcastles on this family beach.
However, it is best known as the scene of many world land-speed record attempts, the last occasion being in 1935 when Sir Malcolm Campbell drove *Bluebird* to an awesome 276mph, thus beating his own record. These days you can still drive along the sands but no faster than 10mph. Alternatively you can rent a ballon-tyred beach-cruiser bicycle.
Continue north till reaching the underpass at Seabreeze Boulevard.

5 HOWARD JOHNSON HOTEL

Just above the underpass is Daytona's oldest surviving hotel, built in 1888 and retaining some original features.
Turn left and left again on to Atlantic Avenue, the resort's main strip.

6 OCEAN CENTER

A modern hi-tech venue for concerts, conferences, conventions and major sporting events.
Continue south on Atlantic Avenue and turn right on to Auditorium Boulevard.

7 PEABODY AUDITORIUM

This is the home of the Daytona Beach Symphony Society and the Daytona Ballet, where classical concerts, ballet and Broadway musicals are staged. The auditorium is renowned for its fine acoustics.
Proceed down South Wild Olive Avenue to Main Street.

8 MAIN STREET

In early March each year this old restored area turns into a raucous street festival celebrating Motorcycle Week. Bikers from all over the state (and beyond) descend on Daytona for races and general revelry.
Return to the Pier.

St Petersburg

More a living city than a mere resort, St Petersburg nevertheless has its share of attractions and is especially pleasant at weekends when its broad streets are relatively free of traffic and parking is easy. (Note: the popular seaside resort of St Petersburg Beach is a quite separate settlement, 12 miles southwest of here.) *Allow a full day.*

Take I–4 West from Orlando towards Tampa. Enter St Petersburg on the I–92 and head south down Fourth Street North. Turn left for Sunken Gardens.

1 SUNKEN GARDENS

The natural sinkhole on this site was drained and landscaped in the 1930s to provide a perfect showcase for an extensive collection of exotic plants and shrubs. The collection is re-invested with 50,000 new items each year and is a blaze of colour whatever the season. The superb Orchid Arbour is a particular favourite.

Continue south on Fourth Street North to Second Avenue North. Turn left and drive down to the busy yacht basin.

2 DEMENS LANDING

This waterfront park and marina was named after the Russian immigrant, Peter Demens, who was largely responsible for creating St Petersburg by bringing his railway into town in 1888.

Leave the car and take a walk along Bayshore Drive.

3 MUSEUM OF FINE ARTS

This acclaimed museum is housed in an exotic Spanish-Colonial influenced building, set in pleasant, well-shaded gardens. Its museum contains a valuable collection of American, European and French Impressionist paintings, as well as Pre-Columbian and Far Eastern exhibits. Close by on Second Avenue is the much smaller collection of the St Petersburg

Historical and Flight One Museum.
Take the complimentary shuttle bus or walk the short distance to the pier (parking facilities for disabled people only).

4 THE PIER

Resembling an inverted pyramid, the five-storey pier is St Petersburg's best-known landmark, especially for mariners. Inside is an aquarium and restaurants.
Return to your car and drive west on Central Avenue or First Avenue North. Turn left on Fourth Street South, then left on 11th Avenue South.

The Pier – good views, good dining

5 SALVADOR DALÍ MUSEUM

This is the world's largest collection of the eccentric Spanish artist's works, including 93 oils and 200 watercolours. In total its 2,000-plus exhibits are insured for $125 million. Well-informed staff host informative and entertaining guided tours which will enable you to see and appreciate Dali's brilliant *trompe l'oeil* and double-image techniques.
Great Explorations is just around the corner.

The best picture house in town

6 GREAT EXPLORATIONS, THE HANDS-ON MUSEUM

This is a popular place with all the family and attempts to explain some of the more accessible 'hows and whys' of science by ingenious 'hands-on' experiments. Avoid weekday mornings when school parties attend.
Return to Orlando via I–92/I–4 East.

SUNKEN GARDENS
Tel: (813) 896–3187. Open: daily 9am–5pm. Admission charge.
MUSEUM OF FINE ARTS
Tel: (813) 896–2667. Open: Tuesday to Saturday 10am–5 pm, Sunday 1–5pm. Admission charge.
ST PETERSBURG HISTORICAL AND FLIGHT ONE MUSEUM
Tel: (813) 894–1052. Open: Monday to Saturday 10am–5pm; Sunday 1–5pm. Admission charge.
SALVADOR DALÍ MUSEUM
Tel: (813) 823–3767. Open: Tuesday to Saturday 9.30am–5.30pm, Sunday noon–5.30pm. Admission charge.
GREAT EXPLORATIONS, THE HANDS-ON MUSEUM
Tel: (813) 821–8992. Open: Monday to Saturday, 10am–5pm; Sunday noon-5pm. Admission charge.

mountains, to compete with his own man-made offerings. Besides which, there are some good white sand beaches (man-made, of course), at Fort Wilderness, and at several hotel resorts. However, these are for Walt Disney World hotel guests only and swimming is forbidden from most of these. You can also swim and lie on the beach at Typhoon Lagoon and River Country or at Wet 'n' Wild, but most of the time these are all too busy to sunbathe in peace

The initial attraction of Florida as a holiday resort was its 1,000-mile coastline of superb sandy beaches. It may therefore seem a little perverse to come all the way to the Sunshine State and stay inland; in fact Orlando is just about as far away from the coast as you can be in Florida!

So why on earth did Walt Disney choose this location? The answer is simple. Walt just did not want any natural attractions, be they beaches or

and they are not designed for proper swimming.

What about all the lakes that dot Central Florida? Yes, there are small beaches on some of these, but in the hot summer months high levels of bacteria cause them to close down and mosquitoes and other insects can make summer country life very unpleasant. Beware if lifeguards are not on duty and never swim in unsigned waters (there may be alligators present!).

LIFE'S A BEACH

So, there may be no alternative but to head for the coast. This isn't such a chore as Cocoa Beach (see pages 106–7) is just 60 miles east and the closest beaches to the west on the Gulf Coast are 100 miles away.

Gulf Coast beaches and resorts are far more attractive than those on the Atlantic coast and two-centre holidays are usually based at either Clearwater or St Petersburg beach; both are part of the 28-mile strip of clean, safe white sands that makes up the famed Pinellas Suncoast.

For even better beaches head a little further south to Sarasota

(127 miles southwest of Orlando) where the soft round white grains of 'sugar sand' provide some of the best sunbathing in the whole state.

Tampa

Like Orlando, Tampa was initially developed around a strategic fort used in the Seminole Indian Wars. Today it is a prosperous city with a mixed economy encompassing various manufacturing and service industries, including brewing, cigars and tourism. *Allow a full day.*

Take the I–4 north to Tampa from Orlando. Exit at the I–275 South junction and take Ashley Drive south to Kennedy Boulevard. Cross Hillsborough River Bridge and enter the university gardens.

1 UNIVERSITY OF TAMPA-HENRY B PLANT MUSEUM

It was the dream of railway millionaire Henry B Plant that the Tampa Bay Hotel, as this extravagant 500-room, neo-Moorish structure once was, should be the finest hotel in the world. To this end, he spent $3 million. Plant filled the place with his personal collection of antiques and Oriental art from all over the world, and installed new-fangled electric lighting and hot and cold running water. Some 4,000 guests stayed in the first season but its success was short-lived. Plant died in 1899 and the hotel closed in 1929. The city snapped it up for just $125,000 and it was converted to the city university. A museum set up in one wing exhibits Plant's collection and tours of the building are also given. *Return to I–275 and head north on to I–4. Go east to the Ybor City exit, south on 21st Street and right on to Palm Avenue. Continue to 13th Street, then turn left for Ybor Square.*

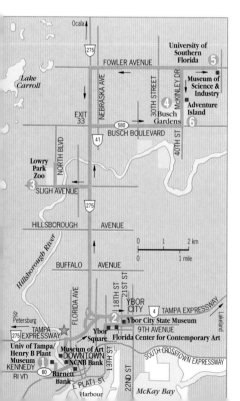

2 YBOR CITY AND SQUARE

Once a cigar factory employing 4,000 people, Ybor Square is now a shopping complex including pavement cafés and restaurants. Ybor City's main street of Seventh Avenue is graced by the ornate

UNIVERSITY OF TAMPA-HENRY B PLANT MUSEUM
Tel: (813) 254–1891. Open: Tuesday to Saturday 10am–4pm, Sunday noon–4pm. Admission charge. Tour reservation, tel: (813) 253–6220.
LOWRY PARK ZOO
Tel: (813) 935–0246. Open: daily 9.30am–5pm (winter), 9.30am–6pm (summer).
MOSI
Tel: (813) 985–5531. Open: Sunday to Thursday 9am–6pm, Friday and Saturday 9am–9pm. Admission charge.
ADVENTURE ISLAND
Tel: (813) 987–5660 for schedule. Open: daily in spring and summer, weekends only in autumn.

Ritz Theater and the 1894 Italian Club, which stands opposite the Florida Center for Contemporary Art. Typical 1890s artisan houses are to be found carefully restored at Preservation Park, on 18th Street. The Harbour Island waterfront leisure and entertainment development on South Harbour Island Boulevard is worth a diversion.
Drive east on Ninth Avenue, left on to 22nd Street and north to rejoin I–4 West. Branch off on to I–275 North then take the Sligh Avenue exit, head west and turn right at North Boulevard.

3 LOWRY PARK ZOO
A free-flight aviary houses dozens of tropical bird species whilst animals too are kept in near-natural conditions. There is also an acclaimed manatee research and rescue centre.
Return to join I–275 North. Turn off after 2 miles at exit 33 on to SR 580 (Busch

Boulevard). Continue for 2 miles to the Busch Gardens entrance on 40th Street (McKinley Drive).

4 BUSCH GARDENS/ ADVENTURE ISLAND
This hugely popular leisure park takes an African safari theme (see pages 116–7). Adjacent is the lively 19-acre water park, Adventure Island.
Head north up McKinley Drive, turn right on to Fowler Avenue, then head east for one mile.

5 MUSEUM OF SCIENCE AND INDUSTRY (MOSI)
This distinctive hi-tech building is festooned with pipes and elevated walkways. It is Florida's largest science centre, featuring some 300 hands-on exhibits to explore, with electronics taking pride of place.
Head west on Fowler Avenue, turn left on to McKinley Drive, 40th Street, which runs south to join the I–4. Head back east on the I–4 to Orlando.

Museum of Science and Industry

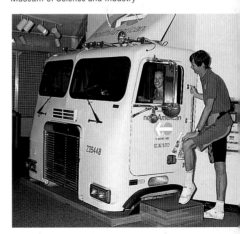

Busch Gardens

*O*utside Orlando, Busch Gardens is the most visited theme park in Florida. And its fiercely loyal devotees would claim that the Gardens beat Disney in appeal. It might be older, less slick or well polished, but it's also less commercial and the wild animals here are decidedly real, not animatronics. However, it's the highly-acclaimed white-knuckle and water rides, rather than a love of nature which draws most visitors.

The eight main themed areas take inspiration from African locations, and the park's official title is Busch Gardens: The Dark Continent. It's a safari worth taking, as you are transported to a Moroccan marketplace, tropical bird gardens, the jungle of the Congo and the African veldt.

BIRD GARDENS

A well-stocked if rather old-fashioned aviary, offering an interesting World of Birds show, starring parrots and birds of prey. This is one of the few chances you will get of seeing the baldheaded eagle – America's national bird.

White Tigers – burning bright!

CONGO

For wildlife lovers the stars of this area are the rare white Bengal tigers on Claw Island. For most adolescents, however, they are a mere sideshow to the thrill-rides. Roller-coaster addicts will make a beeline for The Python, which twists its way through two complete 360-degree spirals, while the Congo River Rapids is a popular white-water raft ride. Be prepared for a soaking (plastic macs are on sale).

CROWN COLONY

A spot to relax in Victorian splendour, with the Crown Colonial House restaurant looking out over the expanse of the Serengeti Plain.

MOROCCO

The eight-piece Mystic Sheiks Band will give you a noisy welcome as you enter this Moorish bazaar-like fantasyland. Here too you will find snake charmers, jugglers, craft shops and the ornate Moroccan Palace – home to the Around The World On Ice spectacular.

NAIROBI

In this area the animals definitely take pride of place. You can see crocodiles and alligators, elephants and much more. There's a special area with simulated night-time conditions, so you can view nocturnal animals, and a petting zoo for children is also featured.

SERENGETI PLAIN

This is the park's oldest section, where giraffes, ostriches, camels and antelopes graze freely and the rare black rhino is being successfully bred.

Splash down – you're in for a soaking on several rides here!

FROM BEER GARDEN TO DARK CONTINENT

Busch Gardens started from very modest beginnings. The gardens were originally a mere hospitality adjunct to brewery tours, with a few flamingos and parrots dotted around for decorative and novelty purposes. Today it's a 300-acre site, housing one of the most important zoological collections in the US and boasting state-of-the-art theme park attractions as well.

Plan to end your day at the brewery where you can see how the brewing process takes place American style and (if you are over 21) sample the beer yourself.

STANLEYVILLE

Water rides predominate here; the Stanley Falls log flume and Tanganyika Tidal Wave both make a very big splash.

TIMBUKTU

All the fun of the fair with the loop-the-loop Scorpion rollercoaster, the Phoenix swingboat motion-sickness nightmare and the fast whirling Sandstorm ride draw long queues.

Busch Garden's latest attraction is the Kumba (it means 'roar'). This is the largest and fastest steel roller coaster in the southeastern United States and features the world's largest loop! *Location: 3000 East Busch Boulevard (at 40th Street), Tampa. Tel: (813) 987–5171. Open: daily 9.30am–6pm (later in summer). Admission charge.*

Cypress Gardens

*T*his charming garden park, opened in 1936, is today the grand-daddy of all Florida's theme parks. It is internationally renowned for its gardens, its thrilling water-ski shows and its good old-fashioned Southern style, personified by the Southern Belles; pretty young ladies who adorn the grounds in their traditional hooped antebellum dresses.

Over 8,000 individual varieties of plants, drawn from some 75 countries, are to be found at this tropical showcase. You can just wander around the gardens or take a slow boat on the Botanical Gardens Cruise. For a bird's-eye view jump aboard the Kodak Island in the Sky, a revolving platform on a huge crane-like arm which hauls its way up from ground level to a height of 153 feet. There's lots more besides plants and girls in the gardens, however. The latest attraction is Wings of Wonder, a huge conservatory housing over 1,000 free-flying butterflies, along with exotic waterfowl and a family of neon-green iguanas. Alligators, snake and parrot shows, a petting zoo ('Hug Haven'), some fairly offbeat small museum collections and a children's playground help fill a very enjoyable family day out.

Floral festivals

Major botanical displays are held at Cypress Gardens throughout the year. From 1 March to 31 May blooms burst forth during the Annual Spring Flower Festival; featuring uniquely created floral displays, from animal topiaries to a kaleidoscope of spring blooms. North America's largest annual chrysanthemum festival, held here each November, showcases more than 2 million blooms in flowering beds and impressively inventive arrangements. Winter is brightened up from 1 December to mid-January by more than 40,000 red, white, pink, speckled and marbled poinsettias, displayed in beds and hanging baskets.

Location: 33 miles south of Orlando, off US19 near Winter Haven. Tel: (813) 324–2111. Open: daily 9.30am–5.30pm (later in summer). Admission charge.

No noise, no fuss, no animatronics – just natural beauty

GETTING AWAY FROM IT ALL

'Florida does beguile and gratify me –
giving me my first and last sense of the
tropics or, à peu pres, the sub-tropics,
and revealing to me a blandness of
nature of which I had no idea.'
HENRY JAMES,
letter to Edmund Goss, 1905

Lakes and Rivers

*L*akes, ponds, creeks, rivers or canals – you are never far from water in Orlando. So, if you want a break from the hurly burly of all those theme parks, the many miles of Florida waterways provide an easy retreat into an altogether slower-paced way of life.

LAKE JESSUP
The marshy fringes of this unspoilt expanse of tranquil water provide a perfect habitat for egrets, herons, ducks and a huge diversity of waterfowl. Surrounded by wetlands, its panorama is best enjoyed from the bridge on SR 46.
Location: 8 miles southeast of Sanford.

LAKE OKEECHOBEE
Look at the map of Florida and the large blue hole just south of centre is Lake Okeechobee. This huge natural reservoir

is the second largest body of freshwater wholly within the US (ie excluding most of the Great Lakes) and measures some 750 square miles in area. It is, however, just 14 feet deep at its lowest point. Lake Okeechobee is also the starting point and primary source of the Everglades, Florida's famous southern swamp region.

Despite its massive size the lake does not appear on early 19th-century maps of the state. The reason for this is that this part of the world was difficult to explore and populated only by native Indians; in fact the Seminole Indians still run a successful cattle operation on the northwestern shores of the lake. Those cartographers who made it as far as the lake simply never made it back to their drawing boards!

Today the lake is something of a haven for birdwatchers and fishermen, particularly for those in search of bass. Otherwise there is little to see here. The lake's only 'town', Okeechobee City, is a small settlement, remarkable only for the commemorative monument to a Seminole Indian victory, which stands just south of town.

LAKE OSCEOLA
Fringed by the elegant park, Lake Osceola, along with neighbouring Lake Maitland and Lake Virginia, provides an enviable waterfront setting for some of the most exclusive homes in Orlando.

Peaceful Lake Maitland, Winter Park

Thanks to canals, which were built to facilitate the logging industry, trips operated by Scenic Boat Tours reach all three lakes (see page 95).
Location: 6 miles northeast of downtown Orlando. East Morse Boulevard, Winter Park.

Perfect start to the day – a dawn catch on Lake Tohopekaliga

LAKE TOHOPEKALIGA
This expansive stretch of water is renowned for such bird species as egrets, herons, pelicans and bald eagles. The lake is well stocked with fish and boats and tackle are for hire at Lake Toho Marina on Lakeshore Boulevard.
Location: Lakeshore Boulevard is 8 miles southeast of Old Town, Kissimmee.

ST JOHN'S RIVER
The St John's is Florida's largest and most important natural waterway and is also one of the very few rivers in the US to flow northwards. This peaceful, lazy ribbon rises near Fort Pierce (some 60 miles south of Cocoa Beach) and meanders for mile upon mile through dense woodlands and windswept marshes for around 250 miles, before curving east through Jacksonville to reach the Atlantic Ocean.

The classic way of enjoying the river is to take a trip aboard the Rivership Romance. All aboard at North Palmetto Avenue, Sanford; tel: (800) 423–7401.

SILVER RIVER
Narrated, four-hour trips unveil 'the real Florida' along the banks of the beautiful Silver River. The ubiquitous cypress, cedar, and giant oak trees provide a ready perch for many species of birds. If you are lucky you might also see raccoons, otters and wild turkeys. If not, head to Silver Springs where there is wildlife (native and introduced) in abundance along the Silver River banks (see page 90).
Reservations required – tel: (407) 298–8011 or (904) 360–8130 for details.

WEKIWA RIVER
Claimed, with some justification, to be Florida's most beautiful natural waterway, the unspoilt backwaters of this slow-flowing river are best discovered from the country store at Katie's Wekiwa River Landing. Motor boat and guided canoeing tours are available.
Location: 22 miles north of Orlando. Katie's Wekiwa River Landing, Sanford. I–4 east to SR 46, head west for five miles to Wekiva Park Drive, a dirt road which leads, in one mile, to the landing. Tel: (407) 628–1482.

BLACK GOLD
The fertile drained Everglades region around Lake Okeechobee is a prime winter fruit and vegetable producer. It is also the land of black gold: not oil, in this case, but sugar cane makes Clewiston the sugar capital of the state. Half the nation's raw sugar consumption (around 1.5 million pounds) is hand-harvested here by Jamaican labourers wielding machettes. Clewiston's other claim to fame is its cabbage palm business, which supplies the fresh hearts of palm dished up in smart Florida restaurants.

DOWN THE LAZY RIVER

There is no better way of exploring the quiet backwaters of Central Florida than in a canoe. If Cinderella's Castle is the symbol of the New Florida then a timeless crystal-clear riverscape of tall cypresses, draped with Spanish moss is quintessential Old Florida. It's a thrill to witness it at Silver Springs or Weeki Wachee, but it's even better to be part of it.

There are many places where you can start paddling. Among the best for beginners are Katie's Wekiwa River Landing (see page 121) and Alexander Springs or Juniper Springs (see page 90) in the Ocala National Forest. Here you can simply float downstream on the gentle current, so you can't get lost and at times you don't even have to paddle, just steer. Lifejackets are provided.

Because a canoe is so quiet you don't scare away the wildlife and as birds and animals have less fear of boats than of people on foot, you can observe them at close hand: egrets, herons, anhingas (see pages 128–9), deer, turtles, otters, raccoons and perhaps bobcats will all make an appearance. You can even get quite close to the alligators – don't worry, they are more scared of you than vice-versa and never attack unless provoked. At the end of the trail, usually after some three to five hours, the canoe-rental company will pick you up at the pre-arranged time and take you back to the start point in a van.

Once you have a little more confidence you can tackle slightly wilder trails. Ask about longer trails with the option of camping overnight. The Ocala National Forest is a canoeist's paradise. Or try one of the State Parks – Blue Spring, León Spring, Lake Kissimmee, Lower Wekiwa River or Wekiwa Springs are all good – or closer to Orlando, Disney's Fort Wilderness. Most, if not all, should be able to supply canoe trail maps and life-jackets.

The other great advantage of canoeing is its price. This can be as little as $2 per hour and is probably the best value activity in the whole state.

If you would like to spend longer on the water, consider renting a houseboat at the Hontoon Landing near De Land. The boats can be taken along the river and you can hire them on a daily basis (tel: (904) 734–2470, or within Florida (800) 248–2474).

Parks and Gardens

Greater Orlando and Central Florida beyond is punctuated by wide open spaces, from formal manicured urban parks and gardens to the wild, but carefully managed Florida State Parks. The latter, of which there are 11 in Central Florida, have been chosen by the state authorities as representative of a particular type of ecosystem and are managed as naturally as possible, giving visitors the chance to explore natural Florida without harming it.

BIG TREE PARK
Big Tree Park is famous for The Senator, a 3,500 year-old bald cypress tree which towers 138 feet high. It was actually 165 feet tall until a hurricane took its top off in 1925. It is one of the oldest and largest trees in the US and over the centuries has been used by Indians, settlers and traders as a landmark.
Location: Longwood, 24 miles north of Orlando. General Hutchinson Parkway. Tel: (407) 323–9165. Open: Monday to Friday 7am–dusk; weekends 9am–dusk. Free.

BLUE SPRINGS STATE PARK
Blue Springs was once a port on the St John's River and its history can be traced in the century-old Thursby House, a former steamboat landing in the park. Today, it is famous as a winter home for Florida's endangered manatees (see pages 92–3) which can usually be seen here from November through March. Recreational activities include camping,

State parks are open daily from dawn to dusk and make a modest entrance charge. For a brochure, write to the Department of Natural Resources, Division of Recreation and Parks, 3900 Commonwealth Boulevard, Tallahassee, FL 32399–3000.

swimming and canoeing in Blue Springs Run and boating and fishing on the St John's River. A ferry will take you to the adjacent 1,650-acre Hontoon Island State Park, formerly a boat yard, a cattle ranch and a pioneer homestead. The first inhabitants of the park were Timucuan Indians whose shell mounds (they were voracious seafood eaters) can still be seen on the park trails. Boating and fishing can be enjoyed here and six authentic rustic cabins are available for adventurous modern-day frontiersmen.
Location: Blue Springs State Park is 2 miles west of Orange City; Hontoon Island is 6 miles west of De Land, off SR 44. Both parks: 2100 West French Avenue, Orange City. Thursby House open: Thursday to Sunday 11am–4pm. Tel: (904) 775–3663. Admission charge.

BOK TOWER GARDENS
This beautiful serene sanctuary in the highlands of Central Florida has been welcoming visitors since 1928. Squirrels, quail and wood ducks roam the expansive grounds and thousands of azaleas, camellias and magnolias provide colour and scent all year round. The remarkable Singing Tower, a 205-foot stone and marble edifice, contains 57 bronze bells. Music rings out tunefully every half hour and a 45-minute carillon recital is played daily at 3pm.
Location: 3 miles north of Lake Wales.

Floral exhibit, Dickson Azalea Park

Off Burns Road (County Road 17A). Tel: (813) 676–1408. Open: daily 8am–5pm. Admission charge.

DICKSON AZALEA PARK

The name says it all, stunning displays of one of Florida's most evocative flowering shrubs make this a popular urban retreat.
Location: 3 miles east of downtown Orlando (Routes 408/436). Open: daily 9am–dusk.

LAKE EOLA PARK

Recently renovated after many years of neglect, this grassy spot in the heart of downtown Orlando is now a favourite spot for all the family. The pleasant walkway round the lake is just under a mile. You can get on to the lake in a charming swan-shaped pedal boat. These are available for rental right up until 8pm (later in high summer) and are a great way of seeing the sunset over the mini-Manhattan skyline of Orlando's business district. On the first Tuesday of each month a free comedy show for all the family, FunnyEola, is performed here.
Location: Robinson Street/Rosalind Avenue. Tel: (407) 246–2827. Open: daily 7am–midnight. Free.

LAKE KISSIMMEE STATE PARK

Kissimmee was once the heart of early Florida's cattle country and at weekends you can see a reconstruction of an 1876 'cow camp' here (see pages 32–7). Moreover, this is the only State Park in Central Florida which is rated as a 'gem' by the Florida State Parks Authority. This means it is officially underutilised and offers camping facilities that give you a real taste of the wild (albeit in reasonable comfort). It also offers outstanding fishing, canoeing and boating opportunities and nature lovers will enjoy the 13 miles of hiking trails along which white-tailed deer, bald eagles, sandhill cranes, turkeys and bobcats are often seen.
Location: Off SR 60, 15 miles east of Lake Wales. 14248 Camp Mack Road, Lake Wales. Tel: (813) 696–1112. Admission charge.

Clowning around at Lake Eola Park

LEU BOTANICAL GARDENS
This glorious refuge close to downtown Orlando is the city's most popular setting for civic functions, weddings and receptions. The park contains Leu House, a picturesque turn-of-the-century Florida farmhouse, now housing an interesting museum which celebrates the lifestyle of local farmers of the 1910-1930 era who cultivated the land. A floral clock, orchids, roses, camellias and azaleas make for lovely walks.

Location: 5 miles north of downtown Orlando. 1730 North Forest Avenue, Orlando. Tel: (407) 246–2620. Open: Tuesday to Saturday 10am–4pm, Sunday to Monday 1–4pm. Admission charge.

MEAD BOTANICAL GARDENS
Rare plants, shrubs and trees enjoy a pleasing lakeland setting amidst the suburban sprawl.
Location: Winter Park (off Route 426) S Denning Avenue. Tel: (407) 623–3334.

ORLANDO PARKS

Open: daily 8am–dusk. Free.

MOSS COUNTRY PARK

Grassy wetlands and open pine woods make up this unspoiled treat within easy reach of Orlando. Wear stout shoes and do not forget to take some refreshment along with you.

Location: 20 miles south of Orlando. On Route 15, 3 miles south off Bee-Line Expressway (Route 528). Open: daily dawn to dusk. Free.

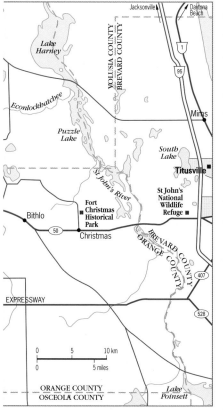

ORLANDO WILDERNESS PARK

This is an artificially created wetland with some 18 miles of dikes and cycle trails. The park is particularly good for birdwatching with year-round viewing of vultures, many species of herons and egrets, bald eagles, limpkins and red-shouldered hawks. Alligators, turtles, raccoons and river otters are also in evidence.

Location: approximately 4 miles northeast of Christmas (25 miles east of Orlando). Tel: (407) 246–2800. Open: daily late January to September. Free.

TURKEY LAKE PARK

A playground designed for handicapped as well as able-bodied children is one of the many worthy features in this pleasant 300-acre park, renowned for its fishing facilities off its 200-foot wooden pier. There are bicycle and hiking trails, canoe rentals, two beaches, a swimming pool and a petting zoo, plus picnic tables, rental cabins and campsites.

Location: 3401 Hiawassee Road, Orlando. Tel: (407) 299–5594. Open: daily 9.30am–7pm. Admission charge.

WEKIWA SPRINGS STATE PARK

An abundance of birds and other wildlife inhabit this untainted and well-managed natural wilderness park. Trails lead through open country, dotted with pine woods where quail, hawks and wood-peckers are readily spotted, along with the ever-present vultures, hovering overhead.

Adjacent to the park is Kelly Country Park which also gives a true sense of being in the great American wilderness.

Location: Route 436, near Apopka (18 miles north of Orlando via US 441, off SR 434 or 436). 1800 Wekiva Circle, Apopka. Tel: (407) 889–9920.

BIRDLIFE

Florida is a favourite spot for birdwatchers and although the Everglades and the Florida Keys are the best known locations, there is still plenty of interest in Central Florida.

Even the smallest ponds, ditches and marshes are likely to host herons and egrets, which thrive on the abundant frogs and fishes. Among the most attractive and distinctive of these is the snowy egret, an aptly named bird with pure white plumage. In common with many of Florida's other birds, they are curiously indifferent to people and can often be watched at close range without being disturbed.

Colourful flamingos, a snowy egret and the unusual anhinga

Altogether less attractive, though no less interesting, are the vultures which can be seen circling overhead almost everywhere in Central Florida. Two species are found here, the black vulture and the turkey vulture. Both have black plumage but the latter has a bald red head. They are bold when feeding and will even descend in search of animal road casualties (armadillos are sadly frequently found squashed by the roadside). However, they are shy in private and their nests are rarely seen.

One of the strangest Florida birds is the anhinga, or 'snakebird', which swims through the water with only its thin, flexible neck above the surface. Anhingas dive to skewer fish on their pointed beaks, surface, flip their catch in the air, retrieve it and swallow it with practised aplomb. Despite its aquatic life-style, the anhinga's feathers are not waterproofed, so it is common to see these birds drying their wings by the water's edge.

Florida's most spectacular native bird, the flamingo, was hunted to extinction in the 19th century, its plumage providing a popular fashion accessory. The creatures which grace Walt Disney World and many other parks today are their Caribbean cousins. They are not even naturally pink anymore. Wild flamingos obtain their rosy hue from their natural shellfish diet but in captivity a pink colouring is simply added to their food!

Pelicans and American black vultures

ALLIGATORS

'Behold him rushing forth from the flags and reeds. His enormous body swells. His plaited tail brandished high. The waters like a cataract descend from his opening jaws, clouds of smoke issue from his dilated nostrils. The earth trembles with his thunder...'
William Bartram, naturalist-explorer, on seeing an alligator fight. *Travels*, 1791.

Today the living raw material for a thriving industry, succulent alligator meat is served in trendy restaurants, cured alligator skins provide fashionable shoes, belts, handbags and blown alligator eggs are collectors' curios. Florida's famous alligators have become a tourist attraction too, though alligator wrestling has always been a somewhat dubious pastime rather than a necessity for man's survival in the swamplands. Contrary to legend, these somewhat shy creatures are not given to attacking people – unless they feel themselves threatened, at which point they are extremely dangerous.

Alligators will eat almost anything – including each other – and feed themselves from birth. Seemingly sluggish and slow moving, they are powerful swimmers and can sprint at high speed for short distances on land, which is why so many waterside homes in Orlando have special fences to keep pet dogs from harm. It is also the reason why you should never approach an alligator in the wild.

Alligators do not hibernate in winter, but tend to hide themselves away in the undergrowth when it is cold. But come the fine weather, they are easy to spot, snoozing on river banks and at lakesides – even on waterways in the middle of urban Orlando, as those taking boat tours from Winter Park are astonished to discover. Even the crowds who flock to Florida's beaches do not enjoy sunbathing as much as these primeval cold-blooded creatures.

Growing up to 12 feet from tip to tail, the Florida alligator is far more common than its endangered cousin, the American crocodile, which prefers the saltwater habitat of the Florida Bay area in the far south of the state.

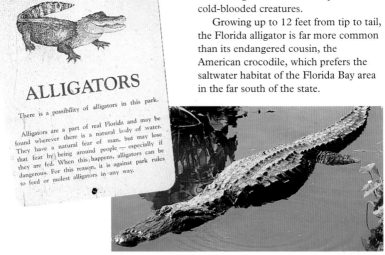

ALLIGATORS

There is a possibility of alligators in this park.

Alligators are a part of real Florida and may be found wherever there is a natural body of water. They have a natural fear of man, but may lose that fear by being around people — especially if they are fed. When this happens, alligators can be dangerous. For this reason, it is against park rules to feed or molest alligators in any way.

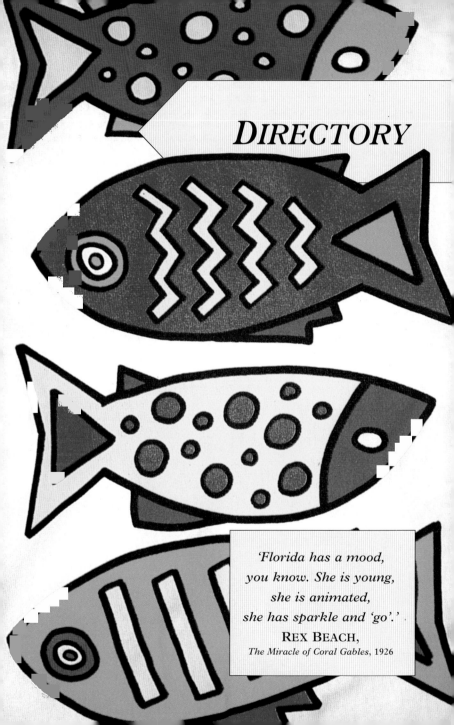

DIRECTORY

'Florida has a mood,
you know. She is young,
she is animated,
she has sparkle and 'go'.'
REX BEACH,
The Miracle of Coral Gables, 1926

Shopping

*F*rom the exclusive high-fashion boutiques of Winter Park to the souvenir bazaars of International Drive, Orlando offers a wide range for most shoppers and, because there is so much competition, prices are generally reasonable. The many malls and shopping villages dotted around town are worth checking out while specialist factory outlet complexes offer big brands at 'factory-direct' prices.

Once you get beyond souvenirs for friends and family, you may want to buy something for yourself.

Cameras represent good value, though model names and numbers may be different in the US, and film is so inexpensive that it is hardly worth bringing any from home. Trendy brand-name sunglasses are around half the price in Europe and American brand-name jeans are so cheap you might end up with several pairs. Orlando might be a bit of a drive from the sea, but the town has a number of surf shops.

Arts and crafts shops abound and most of the merchandise is good quality. America likes to present its culinary creations in style and you will find exquisite tableware (even if much of it is imported), as well as everything for the kitchen, including designer bottles of oil and high quality utensils. If you want a better view of it all, it is worth having a sight test – spectacles are much cheaper than at home.

SHOPPING COMPLEXES

Church Street Station Exchange

Downtown's favourite tourist spot offers more than 50 speciality shops and an international food court, all undercover in Victorian-revival surroundings. Look in at The Gothic Shop, with its mind-boggling architectural accessories and more portable knick-knacks, while Gold 'n' Time has a serious selection of good-quality watches. Elsewhere in the complex are sports shops, fashion outlets and a Western *memorabilia* store (see pages 144–5).
129 West Church Street, Orlando. Tel: (407) 422–2434. Open: daily 11am–11pm.

Disney Village Marketplace

Disney merchandise, of course, with enough Mickey Mouses and Donald Ducks to last a lifetime. Mickey's

Orlando's elegant mall

Searching for souvenirs – shopping in Church Street Station

Character Shop is the largest Disney merchandise shop in the world – quality is very good, prices are astronomic. Other outlets offer some classy non-Disney designer clothing and other famous-name goods. You can also watch artisans at work.
Disney World Resort, Lake Buena Vista. Tel: (407) 824–4321. Open: daily 9.30am–10pm.

Florida Mall
This is a typical American suburban shopping mall with a good range of shops and department stores. A walk round the supermarket can be fun – comparing branding and pricing and picking up some of those speciality food items which are still a bit hard to find in Europe.
Location: 5 miles east of International Drive. 8001 South Orange Blossom Trail, Orlando. Tel: (407) 851–6255. Open: Monday to Saturday 10am–9pm, Sunday 11am–6pm.

Mercado Mediterranean Village
More than 50 shops and boutiques offer a wide range of goods, all in a pleasant

ORLANDO MAGICARD
Ring (800) 551–0181 or call at the Orlando Visitors Center at Mercado Mediterranean Village, 8445 International Drive (open: 8am–8pm) for a free Orlando Magicard which offers discounts of 10 to 50 per cent at many of the city's shops (and at restaurants and attractions too).

Italianate setting. Look for the specialist Coca Cola *memorabilia* shop, along with great belt buckles, baseball caps and shirts and leather jackets.
8445 South International Drive, Orlando. Tel: (407) 345–9337. Open: daily 10am–10pm.

Orlando Fashion Square
Dedicated followers of fashion can choose from 165 stores, including popular US department stores such as JC Penney, Sears and other big names.
Location: 3 miles east of I–4. 3201 East Colonial Drive, Orlando. Tel: (407) 896–1131. Open: Monday to Saturday 10am–10pm, Sunday noon–5.30pm.

This is the place to come to pick up goods at bargain prices

FACTORY OUTLETS

These downmarket malls may not be the most glamorous places to shop, but with discounts of up to 75 per cent off normal shop prices, hardened bargain hunters grit their teeth and get right down to it.

Belz Factory Outlet

This is Orlando's largest discount shopping centre, comprising around 170 stores. With big names like Calvin Klein, Reebok, OshKosh, Van Heusen, Jordache, Bally and Lee prominent, it is just the place to find quality trainers, men's, women's and children's fashion wear, luggage and jewellery all at bargain basement prices.
5401 W Oakridge Road (north end of International Drive), Orlando. Tel: (407) 352–9611.

Kissimmee Manufacturer's Outlet Mall

Nike, Van Heusen and Reebok are just some of the brands to feature at ex-

factory prices in the 20 or so shops in this busy mall.
Old Vineland Road, Kissimmee. Tel: (407) 396–8900.

MARKETS

True street markets are few and far between, particularly in Orlando itself where discount shopping is covered by factory outlet stores. 'Flea markets' are also often misnomers in European terms, being small shops selling new items, rather than market stalls dealing in second-hand goods. The following all have something to offer though.

Flea World

This is the biggest flea market in Central Florida with around 1,600 booths. It opens from Friday through Sunday, selling anything and everything from pet spiders to kinky underwear and of course lots of Disney-lookalike merchandise. Within the complex is Fun World, a small fairground-style park for children.

*US 17–92 (4 miles southeast of I–4 exit 50)
near Sanford. Tel: (407) 321–1792.*

Osceola Flea and Farmer's Market
Around 900 booths, under cover, sell
new and second-hand merchandise every
weekend, with the emphasis on antiques,
collectibles and Florida souvenirs. There
is another Farmers' Market near by on
Kissimmee Broadway every Thursday.
*E Irlo Bronson Memorial Highway. Tel:
(407) 846–2811.*

Renninger's Antique Center
Set in the delightful village of Mount
Dora (which also holds several good craft
and antique shops) this claims to be the
largest selection of antiques and
collectibles in the whole state. Here,
every weekend, you can choose from 150
to 200 booths. Adjacent is Renninger's
Farmers' and Flea Market where fresh
foods and second-hand items are sold.

Antique Fairs held bi-monthly swell
the number of stallholders to nearer 500,
while 'Extravaganzas', held three times a
year, can double the number again!
*US 441, Mount Dora. Tel: (407)
383–8393 (Thursday to Sunday only).*

Winter Park Farmer's Market
This long-established market meets every
Saturday morning to trade fruit,
vegetables, plants, herbs and other fresh
produce. Breads and pastries are also on
sale. This is a fine place to catch the
neighbourhood spirit of this rather posh
suburban community.
*West Lynam and New York Avenue,
Winter Park. Tel: (407) 623–3334.*

SHOPPING STREETS
International Drive
The pulsating artery of Orlando's
tourism industry, International Drive

offers plenty of opportunity to shop till
you drop – and then come back for
more.

Old Town (Kissimmee)
A Victorian-themed shopping boulevard
featuring around 70 small speciality
shops and lots of other family diversions.
*Highway 192, Kissimmee. Tel: (800)
331–5093 (in Florida).*

Park Avenue, Winter Park
Enjoy relaxed and refined shopping in
the sophisticated and genteel atmosphere
of Orlando's most elegant suburb. This
is a great place to find those really special
little gifts, with shops ranging from a
superb kitchen provisions store, to high
fashion clothing, boutique jewellers and
interior design outlets offering delightful
ornaments, mirrors and clocks. Normal
neighbourhood shopping hours apply,
though some shops also open on Sunday
afternoon.
Winter Park. Tel: (407) 644–8281.

Entertainment and Nightlife

*W*hen the theme parks have closed for the day and the kids are all tucked up safely in bed, there's still plenty happening all over the world's fun capital. Disney's dazzling Pleasure Island entertainment complex and the show bars of Church Street Station are the two strongest magnets but there's plenty more besides. Local nightlife has blossomed all over the area in the past decade.

Many bars offer free admission and live music – and don't forget the dramatically reduced prices of early-evening 'happy hour'. Drinking is generally inexpensive, so leave the car behind and use the reasonably priced taxi cabs.

Though there are not many night-spots which match the sophistication of those found in major cities and other big resorts, many hotels now have their own nightclub operation where you can be entertained and dance the night away.

Rules covering under-age drinking are very strictly enforced. It is illegal for under 21s to drink alcohol and those who are 21 but perhaps look younger will need to produce their passport or some other similar form of identity to prove their age.

For all nightclub listings look in the free Orientations magazine (found in hotel rooms) and in the local paper, *The Orlando Sentinel*.

CINEMA
Several shopping malls include comfortable, modern cinemas where you can catch all the latest Hollywood offerings, usually months before they cross the Atlantic. Check the local press for times and locations. Certification follows very similar lines to that found in the UK and is more strictly enforced.

NIGHTCLUBS AND BARS
Church Street Station
Downtown's major entertainment complex, offering a dazzling array of themed-show bars at a reasonable all-in admission fee (see pages 144–5).

Crocodile Club
Essentially a music bar with dancing (to current dance and chart hits), the Crocodile Club is a smart place to mix

In line for fun

Al fresco entertainment at the Mercado Mediterranean Village

with the young sophisticates of Winter Park and the students from Rollins College from Thursday to Saturday nights.
Bailey's Restaurant, 118 West Fairbanks Avenue, Winter Park. Tel: (407) 647–8501.

Fat Tuesday

Two lively bars, claiming to feature the world's largest choice of frozen daiquiris and providing good live entertainment most nights a week with no cover charge.
310 Park Avenue, Winter Park. Tel: (407) 647–8719. 41 West Church Street, Orlando. Tel: (407) 843–6104.

Giraffe Lounge

This (along with the Laughing Kookaburra) is one of the two busiest nightspots in the Disney complex for locals, Disney staff and those who are bored by Pleasure Island. Its small size adds to its packed atmosphere and live bands play five times a week.
Hotel Royal Plaza, Lake Buena Vista. Tel: (407) 828–2828.

Hilarities Comedy Theater

This is Orlando's showcase for the best in local humour. Wednesday is a non-smoking night, which until recently would have seemed funny in itself. If you fancy a turn at the microphone make a note in your diary that Monday is amateur night. Beware though – there are wise-cracking professionals on hand to heckle!
5351 International Drive. Tel: (407) 363–1920. Minimum age 21. Reservations required.

J J Whispers

JJs has been Orlando's best-known club for some years now and so its outrageous stance has almost taken on an air of respectability. It's basically a state-of-

Ballet at the Bob Carr Performing Arts Center – venue for a variety of entertainment

the-art disco offering different music for different people (including thirty-somethings) on different nights. At weekends it is also home to Bonkerz comedy club. Telephone ahead or see the local press to find out what's on. *5100 Adanson Street, Orlando. Tel: (407) 629-4779.*

Laughing Kookaburra
Good Time Bar

A popular hotel nightclub where locals, hotel guests and Disney staff get down to seventies disco and the latest hits. Live bands start at 10pm. *Buena Vista Palace Hotel, Lake Buena Vista. Tel: (407) 843-2934.*

PLEASURE ISLAND

There's something for everyone at Walt Disney World's nightlife complex and you can even take the children along to some of the clubs.

Sloppy Joe's

An atmospheric Ernest Hemingway inspired hang-out, featuring live music every night, a 4–7pm happy hour from Monday to Friday, authentic Florida Keys food and brain-numbing cocktails. *41 West Church Street, Orlando. Tel: (407) 843-5825.*

Sullivan's Trailways Lounge

Good ol' Southern country and western music and dancing is the draw here with local and big-name live bands doing their 'thang'. You can learn to dance country-style for free on certain nights. *1108 South Orange Blossom Trail (US 441). Tel: (407) 843-2934.*

THE PERFORMING ARTS

On the highbrow scale of performing arts Orlando comes predictably pretty low, with dinner theatre for tourists being the most popular form of entertainment. However, don't write off the possibility of a more cultured night too quickly. Orlando's ballet and opera companies and the Florida State Orchestra all use the Bob Carr Performing Arts Center, tel: (407) 646–2145. This is also the venue for Broadway series and various other quality shows.

Within Greater Orlando, Rollins College, in Winter Park, is home to music and theatre, and has regular recitals and concerts (often free) in the Cornell Fine Arts Museum galleries, tel: (407) 646–2233. Its Annie Russell Theater, tel: (407) 646–2145, has an ambitious summer repertory season and a winter programme. The adjacent Knowles Chapel is a lovely setting for music, with an annual Bach festival (tel: (407) 646–2115).

Keep an eye on who is appearing at the Orlando Arena. Many big names visit here and ticket prices for concerts are often cheap by European standards.

NIGHT CREATURES

Night-time in Orlando doesn't necessarily mean nightclubs, discos or dinner theatre. In summer many theme parks open very late and you can play mini-golf or drive a go-kart until midnight at several places. However, the strangest of all the many options available (which involves scaring yourself silly and probably guarantees nightmares) is ironically a recent European import.

Terror on Church Street comes fresh from the Spanish costas and is a haunted house with 'real' monsters. Besides terrifying special effects you'll meet and be chased by actors playing, among others, Dracula, Freddie Kruger, Norman ('Psycho') Bates and Hannibal Lecter. It could give a whole new meaning to 'just going out for a bite!'

You'll find this horror haven open from 7pm to midnight or later nightly (except Monday) on West Church Street, downtown near Church Street Station. The minimum age limit is 10. Tel: (407) 649–3327.

DINNER SHOWS

Dinner shows have become an Orlando institution. They may not be to everyone's taste, but these casual and hammy fun nights out provide an opportunity to let your hair down, with audience participation an integral part of the proceedings. If you're shy about participating you might want to choose a seat a few rows back, but you will still be expected to forget your inhibitions.

The mass-catered food is generally pretty high on quantity and low on quality, but the actual dining is a mere appetiser to the show itself. Expect to pay around $30 which usually includes as much beer, wine and soft drinks as you like. Book as far ahead as possible.

Arabian Nights

This award-winning show features 50 superbly groomed horses – from Lippizans and quarter horses to Arabians, worth a total $4.5 million. Highlights include a breathtaking re-creation of the chariot race from *Ben Hur*.
6225 West Irlo Bronson Highway, Kissimmee. Tel: (407) 396–7400.

Asian Adventure

A five-course Chinese feast accompanies a two-hour spectacular, starring acrobats, martial arts, and 'The Happy Chef', who keeps 25 plates spinning at once.

DISNEY DINNER THEATER

Three of the most popular shows in Orlando are predictably staged within Walt Disney World. Broadway at the Top has the simple revue theme of its title. It costs half as much again as a typical Orlando dinner show but few visitors complain about value (Contemporary Resort. Tel: (407) 934–7639). From the sublime to the ridiculous, the laugh-a-minute Hoop-Dee-Doo-Revue is Disney at its corniest (Fort Wilderness Resort. Tel: (407) 934–7639) while the Polynesian Luau ('feast') is an outdoor barbecue accompanied by twangy guitars and Hawaiian dancers (Polynesian Resort. Tel: (407) 934–7639).

All these shows are extremely popular so book ahead as soon as you know your holiday dates.

King Henry's Feast

5225 International Drive, International Station, Orlando. Tel: (407) 354–3307.

Blazing Pianos
Many people rate this loose interpretation of the world's most famous festival top of the Orlando dinner shows. Cool New Orleans jazz mixes with red-hot Latin beats and the food is simple but good.
Mercado Mediterranean Village, International Drive, Orlando. Tel: (407) 351–5151.

Capone's
A Broadway-style musical comedy with a gangster theme and a groaning Italian buffet table.
Highway 192, 1 mile east of SR535, Kissimmee. Tel: (407) 397–2378.

King Henry's Feast
The rumbustuous era of the Tudors is recalled in this extravaganza, featuring duelling knights, comedy turns, magicians and speciality acts.
8984 International Drive, Orlando. Tel: (407) 351–5151.

Mark II Dinner Theatre
Musicals and comedy shows are presented while you dine in relaxed comfort. The quality of the show can be variable, with a lot depending on the strength of the audience participation. Not one for the children.
3376 Edgewater Drive, Orlando. Tel: (407) 843–6275.

Medieval Times
Turning the clock back to AD1093, Medieval Times serves a hearty four-course meal on pewter plates while guests watch knights in armour spur their steeds into combat. Daring tournament games recreate the chivalrous spirit of the joust.
4510 Irlo Bronson Highway, Kissimmee. Tel: (407) 396–1518.

Plantation Dinner Theater
Broadway-style productions are on the menu in this old Southern-style theatre restaurant. The food is said to be the best of all Orlando's dinner shows.
Orlando Heritage Inn, 9861 International Drive, Orlando. Tel: (407) 352–0008.

Sleuths
While enjoying their meal, guests act as detectives in solving an intriguing 'who dunnit?' mystery.
Republic Square, Orlando. Tel: (407) 363–1985.

Wild Bill's Wild West Dinner Show
See how the West was won, with demonstrations of rifle shooting, roping, and other cowboy skills, along with a guest appearance of the feared Commanche Indians.
US 192, Kissimmee. Tel: (407) 351–5151.

Equestrian thrills at Arabian Nights

bedtime story and explore a crazy treasure-house packed full of junk, *memorabilia* and special effects. The shows tend to be pretty silly, but then what would you expect?

8 Traxs
Saturday Night fever from the 1970s can be caught every night in this loud pulsating disco club.
Guests must be 21 or over.

Comedy Warehouse
Overseas visitors might find some of the American humour either too parochial or lacking in subtlety but, if you are in the mood, there's plenty of laughter to be had from a mix of solid professional and enthusiastic amateur comedians.

Mannequins
Cleverly designed dancing dummies give their name to this wild disco with its hi-tech, state-of-the-art light show, pulsating music, bubble machine and rotating dancefloor.
Guests must be 21 or over.

Neon Armadillo
Nashville comes to Orlando, with a good standard of live and recorded country music, accompanied by an appropriately 'hicksville' ambience and foaming glasses of beer with Jack Daniels chasers.

Pleasure Island Jazz Company
A new 240-seat venue presenting the best in modern and traditional live jazz plus rhythm 'n' blues.

Rock 'n' Roll Beach Club
One for golden-oldie addicts, with bands of yesteryear doing their best to re-create

PLEASURE ISLAND
Topping off a busy day round the theme parks, Walt Disney World has the nightlife scene covered too, with its own lavish after-dark rendezvous. Occupying a six-acre site, Pleasure Island is built around 19th-century sail-lofts and warehouses (all fake, of course). Seven individually themed and targeted night clubs offer up an endless musical diet of everything from country and western to contemporary rock and dance. The complex is located adjacent to the Walt Disney World Marketplace, reached via catwalks over the lagoon. This puts it within a few minutes stroll of most Disney hotels – quite an advantage for those who want to leave the car behind so they can make a night of it.

Adventurers' Club
An alternative to bopping the night away. Here you can listen to a far-fetched

hits from the '50s, '60s and '70s. In addition to the clubs, there's plenty of street entertainment, a selection of novelty shops, and some good eating places and bars.

The permanently-anchored *Empress Lilly*, a reproduction Mississippi paddle-steamer, offers four pleasant restaurants, while Maxwell's Diner will please lovers of junk food, and Fireworks Factory offers acceptable barbecue fodder and an expansive cocktail list. Cine fans who can't wait for the very latest releases to cross the Atlantic will enjoy the comfortable 10-screen cinema (separate admission from rest of attractions).

Admission to Pleasure Island is free until the clubs open at 7 pm, after which a reasonably-priced pass covers admission to all of the clubs. And, as the various shows and band slots last around 30 minutes and are staged at frequent intervals, you can catch them all in one

evening then simply dance on until closing time.

While under-18s are admitted to most venues, they must be accompanied by an adult and, under Florida state law, alcohol must not be served to anyone under the age of 21. Those who look young for their age should carry some form of ID.

Nighclubs open: 7pm–2am. Shops open: 10am–midnight; restaurants open 11.30am–midnight.

PLANET HOLLYWOOD

Adjacent to Pleasure Island is Orlando's latest famous-name restaurant. Headed by Sylvester Stallone, Arnold Schwarzenegger and Bruce Willis, this all-American hero rendezvous is packed with movie *memorabilia* and features holograms of film stars as well as serving good food. *Tel: (407) 363–7827. No reservations.*

Good ol' boys playing country 'n' western at the Neon Armadillo

CHURCH STREET STATION

Fun is a serious business at Church Street Station. This old hotel depot, once a major stop on the South Florida Railroad, has been painstakingly restored to become Orlando's leading night-time entertainment centre.

The craftsmanship and magpie-like quality of it all is very impressive. Among the many valuable fixtures and fittings you'll see is 250,000 feet of golden lumber from a century-old Ohio barn; ornate chandeliers which once graced the Philadelphia Mint; a solid rosewood pool table dating from 1885; 12-foot-high, hand-carved 18th-century Viennese mirrors and a wine cabinet from a Rothschild townhouse in Paris.

The complex includes a themed shopping mall, restaurants and in homage to its past, railway pushcarts and Old Duke, a 140-ton steam engine.

Restaurants

Food for all tastes, and in a range of price brackets, is offered here. Try the Exchange Food Pavilion for above-average fast food; visit the Cuban Café for exotic Cuban sandwiches, soups and salads; Rosie O'Grady's serves 'red hots' (speciality hot dogs) in its Gay '90s Sandwich Parlour; fresh Florida seafood

At Rosie O'Grady's those who can, can-can

and a choice of pasta are on the menu at Crackers Oyster Bar; buffalo burgers, as well as barbecue pork, beef and chicken are served with all the country fixin's at The Cheyenne Barbecue Restaurant, and Lili Marlene's Aviator's Pub and Restaurant is renowned for its carefully aged beef and fresh seafood, albeit at a price.

Shopping

An eclectic range of shopping for everyone; some of the best Americana souvenirs in town; everything from fashion clothing to cowboy clothing; Victorian bric-à-brac and much more is to be found here. Look in, too, at The Wine Cellar which features over 5,000 bottles of fine wine on its list and holds daily tastings. Window shoppers can have just as much fun and the strolling crowds are part of the ambience.

Station Exchange

Aside from the shops and restaurants (see above), Commander Ragtime's Midway of Fun, Food and Games is a mecca for video games' addicts with its mix of hi-tech challenges and circus ephemera. Suspended from the ceiling is some 1,400 feet of track around which six model trains race. Antique vehicles, replica World War I planes and a beautiful model of the *Queen Elizabeth* ocean liner are other curious items of décor.

Showrooms

Whatever your taste in music, there are good times to be had for a reasonable

Cool jazz at Rosie O'Grady's

admission charge in Church Street Station's five spectacular showrooms. Be prepared for waiting staff dancing on the tables and not-always-willing 'volunteers' being dragged on stage to co-star in the show. Choose between strummin' banjos, Dixieland jazz and Charleston dancers in Rosie O'Grady's Good Time Emporium; live music from the 1950s to the 1990s at the Victorian-styled Orchid Garden Ballroom; Grand Ol' Opry-style country singing at The Cheyenne Saloon and Opera House; or the latest dance sounds at Phineas Phogg's Balloon Works, where the décor features historic lighter-than-air flights. If all you need is a cool refreshing drink, try Apple Annie's Courtyard.

The entertainments at Church Street are ebullient affairs, and generally the complex appeals to young adults, but aside from Phineas Phogg's (minimum age 21), there is hardly anything you could not take an older child to. The shows start at around 7pm and are timed so you can catch several in an evening. *Open: daily shops and restaurants 11am–midnight, showrooms 7pm–2am.*

The Good Time Gazette, detailing all of Church Street's attractions, is available by calling (407) 422–2434.

Festivals and Events

*T*here's a year-round calendar of indoor and outdoor events throughout Central Florida across the sporting, arts, cultural and social spectrum. Updated listings are published regularly in *The Orlando Sentinel* newspaper and in the free *TV & Visitors Guide*, which is distributed in hotel rooms.

JANUARY

Carillon Festival: Tuneful bell-ringing at Bok Tower Gardens. Tel: (813) 676–1408.

Florida Citrus Bowl: Major college American football teams compete in this post-season challenge event on New Year's Day. Tel: (407) 423–2476.

Scottish Highland Games: The Central Florida Fairgrounds in Orlando hosts a Gaelic celebration of traditional sport, food and music. Tel: (407) 339–3335.

FEBRUARY

Daytona 500: Enjoy the thrills of 200mph car and motorcycle racing round the world-renowned high-speed bowl. Tel: (904) 253–RACE.

Kissimmee Valley Livestock Show and Osceola County Fair. Tel: (407) 846–6046.

Mount Dora Art Festival: Held over first or second week of February. Tel: (904) 383–2165.

Silver Spurs Rodeo: Silver Spurs Arena, Kissimmee. Cowboys from all over the south attend this famous long-established event, held at the end of the month. Tel: (407) 847–5000.

MARCH

Bach Festival: A celebration of the great composer at Winter Park's Rollins College. Tel: (407) 646–2182.

Central Florida Fair: Held at the Central Florida Fairgrounds in Orlando.

Tel: (407) 295–3247.

Kissimmee Bluegrass Festival: Hillbilly music throughout the first or second week of the month. Tel: (407) 896–6641.

Nestlé Invitational Golf Classic: Hosted at Bay Hill over the third weekend of the month. Tel: (407) 876–2888.

Spring Floral Festival: Held at Cypress Gardens. Tel: (813) 324–2111. Winter Park Sidewalk Art Festival. Tel: (407) 644–8281.

APRIL

Arts in April: A month-long general festival held throughout Orlando. Tel: (407) 246–2555.

Fountainview Fine Crafts Festival: Lake Eola. Tel: (407) 422–7649.

Orlando Sentinel Book Fair: Literary event at Lake Eola. Tel: (407) 420–5038.

Shakespeare Festival: Lake Eola Ampitheater (until early May). Tel: (407) 423–6905.

JUNE

Miss Florida Pageant: Admire the beauties at the Bob Carr Performing Arts Centre in Orlando. Tel: (407) 849–2577.

JULY

Pepsi 400 NASCAR race: Daytona International Speedway, early in the month. Tel: (904) 253–RACE.

Picnic in the Park: 4 July Independence Day, with fireworks at

Orlando offers a full and varied cultural calendar

many venues, most notably Walt Disney World (huge crowds), Kissimmee Lakefront Park, Lake Eola and Cypress Gardens.

SEPTEMBER
Osceola Art Festival: Kissimmee, mid-month. Tel: (407) 957–4656.
Puerto Rican Parade: Festival Park. Tel: (407) 277–2829.

OCTOBER
Disney in the Park: Lots of fun at Lake Eola, late in the month. Tel : (407) 957–4656.
Florida State Air Fair: Spectacular flying displays at Kissimmee Municipal Airport, early in the month. Tel: (407) 847–4600.
Maitland Art Festival: Lake Lily, mid-month. Tel: (407) 263–5218.
Winter Park Autumn Art Festival: Rollins College, many attractions held mid-month. Tel: (407) 644–8281.

NOVEMBER
Disney's Festival of the Masters: An exhibition by top artists at Walt Disney World Village, first or second weekend. Tel: (407) 824–4531.
Holiday Winterfest: Arts and crafts celebration at Lake Tohopekaliga, Kissimmee. Tel: (407) 860–0092.
Light Up Orlando: Downtown evening street festival, mid-month. Tel: (407) 648–4010.

DECEMBER
Central Florida Art Show: Mount Dora Center for the Arts, December to January. Tel: (904) 383–0880.
Christmas Boat Parade: Lake Tohopekaliga, Kissimmee. Tel: (407) 847–2033.
St Cloud Art Festival: Early December. Tel: (407) 847–5000.

Children

Since most of Orlando's myriad attractions were originally created with children foremost in mind, it's not surprising that the resort is fully geared up to coping with their special needs – and those of their sometimes harassed and distraught parents.

All the major theme parks operate lost-child services, most rent out strollers and buggies and all have specific play areas (even the water parks have safe facilities for those who are only old enough to just paddle and splash around). Toddlers might well be upset when they find they are too small to qualify for some of the more scary rides but the cookie does crumble both ways. Just as there is often a minimum height on some rides there also maximum height restrictions on attractions specially designed for the under-fives.

Health risks

Beware the Florida sunshine at all times. Keep little ones covered up and use the highest protection sun blocks. Don't take small children out into parkland in the high summer. Mosquitoes are a real nuisance to adults let alone children.

Stress

You have paid a lot of money, travelled a long way, and your expectations are high. The children are excited, and terribly overtired. You have paid an arm and a leg for theme park passes, but you only have a few days to spare, and there is an awful lot to see. The queues look

Pluto greets his young fans

Duck-bill hats are fun to wear and keep the sun off the kids

awesome, and the sun beats down. Somehow, you must fight your way in and enjoy yourselves. This is just the time for trouble. No sooner through the turnstiles, than the wails begin.

The sheer size and scale of Orlando's attractions can place a lot of pressure on small children – and their keepers. Rule one – get them in a good frame of mind before you start. Keep things relaxed and low key. You may plan the day with military precision, but don't convey this to the kids. Also try not to cram too much into one day. Be realistic with the time you have. Make an early start, but don't worry if everyone needs a break at some point. Have lunch, or if practical, leave the parks altogether and go back to your hotel for a swim and a rest. You can return later if you get a hand-stamp of invisible fluorescent ink as you leave.

Finally, forget shopping in the theme parks, you can do it later in the evening, or on another day and probably a lot cheaper too.

Spectator Sports

*T*here's no finer way to capture the essence of the real America than at a ball game. Sport is very much a family-day out for Americans and they demand the best facilities – from ample parking and comfortable seating to refreshments brought right to the seats. Orlando caters admirably for sports fans. Stadiums and facilities are top class and spectators are highly partisan but also demonstrate a good humour.

AMERICAN FOOTBALL

The city's premier football team is the Orlando Predators who play at the Orlando Arena (see page 25). College games are listed in the local press and attract an enthusiastic following. The rules are a bit confusing to newcomers but you will find your fellow spectators only too happy to explain the intricacies of the game to you and to expound on why their team is the best.

BASEBALL

The Florida Marlins, founded in 1993, is currently the only major league baseball team in Florida, but future big-time stars play minor league baseball throughout the Greater Orlando area. There are four local 'class A' teams who play in the Florida State League; Baseball City Royals (affiliated to Kansas City) who play in the Baseball City Complex near Haines City (tel: (813) 424–2500); Osceola Astros (affiliated to Houston) who play at Osceola County Stadium, Kissimmee (tel: (407) 933–5500); the Cleveland Indians affiliate team who play in Winter Haven (tel: (813) 293–3900); and the Detroit Tigers affiliate team who play at the Joker Marchant Stadium (tel: (813) 499–8229). Games are very popular, so arrive early to get a good seat.

BASKETBALL

Orlando Arena hosts the Orlando Magic, the local professional basketball team. Games are held regularly (tel: (407) 896–2442) for an up-to-date schedule.

EQUESTRIAN SPORTS

Many of the nation's leading trotters and pacers use the Ben White Raceway, at Orlando Centroplex as their winter training quarters (tel: (407) 849–2000).

GOLF

Major pro-golf events, like the Nestlé Invitational, are held at Bay Hill, just one of several superbly designed and maintained courses dotted around the Orlando area.

JAI ALAI

Pronounced 'high-a-lie' this is one of the world's fastest-moving ball games and

---

TV SPORT

Sport is a major programming item on American television, as a flick through the channels will soon reveal. The only trouble is, coverage tends to be dominated by events being staged in the USA, often with exclusively American participation. American football, baseball, basket ball, ice hockey, boxing and motor sports all get prime-time exposure.

derives from the Spanish Basque sport of pelota. Like tennis it is played either in singles by two players, or in doubles by four players. The court, or fronton, on which it takes place, is rather like a squash court. Using a basket-like glove strapped to the wrist, the players catch and hurl a ball at speeds of up to 188mph. Although the game itself is an exciting spectacle (the rules aren't too difficult to pick up) betting is the main priority among most of the spectators.

The Orlando Seminole Jai Alai fronton is at Fern Park, north of Orlando. Tel: (407) 331–9191.

MOTOR RACING

Daytona International Speedway offers regular race meetings, climaxing each February in the Speedweeks festival. The highlight of this is the famed Daytona 500 stock-car race in which speeds of 190mph are attained on the steeply banked oval track. Crowds are huge – make sure you take plenty to drink and have adequate protection for several hours spent broiling in the sun. Other major events hosted at the Speedway include the Pepsi 400, the World Car Endura Kart race and an important pro-am cycling event.

SOCCER

As a host city for the World Cup, Orlando went soccer mad during summer 1994. Thanks to the facilities offered by the 72,000-seat Florida Citrus Bowl stadium – including $4.6 million worth of improvements – the Florida location was chosen as one of nine host cities from 27 applicants. Soccer is increasingly popular in schools and colleges, though, at present, Orlando does not have a professional side.

Orlando's breathtaking Citrus Bowl

THE MECCA OF SPEED

There was a time in the early years of the century when monstrous racing cars pounded down the sands of Daytona Beach in a frenzied quest for the world land-speed record. Racing started at the beach back in 1902 but eventually the large crowds and construction along the seafront made it too dangerous. In 1959 it moved to the purpose-built Daytona International Speedway – a hallowed venue which today hosts a greater variety of motor racing events than any other track in the world.

The 450-acre, high-banked oval track is a veritable temple of speed. Of course, there's nothing to beat a big race day, when the grandstands are jam-packed with an expectant crowd of thousands and the intoxicating smells of racing fuel and hot dogs mix in the air. The biggest is Daytona 500 day when 40 brave stock-car competitors hurtle round at speeds up to 190mph.

On non-race days, visitors can take a leisurely guided tour of the complex, watch footage from old racing films, study the historic still photographs and *memorabilia* in the Gallery of Legends and even be literally driven round the wall, before indulging their enthusiasm in the Pit Shop. Special events, such as guest appearances by leading drivers, live broadcasts from the grandstand of Eli Gold's NASCAR Live MRN radio show and other family-orientated entertainment make for a packed day.

Near by on West International Speedway Boulevard is the Klassix Auto Museum with more than 100 classic cars including a rare 1953 Chevrolet Corvette, Ford Mustangs, Dodge Chargers and Porsches, tel: (804) 252–3800.

Life in the fast lane – Daytona style

Participant Sports

*C*entral Florida has an enviable number of first-rate sporting facilities, with more than 40 golf courses, 21 tennis centres, over 800 tennis courts plus jogging trails, cycle routes and horse riding stables.

CYCLING
A number of cycle shops located throughout the Orlando area offer mountain bike hire at reasonable rates and there are a variety of cycle trails to be explored.

FISHING
Given the large number of streams, rivers, lakes and canals and its proximity to both the Atlantic and Gulf coasts, Orlando is an angler's paradise. Freshwater fishermen require a licence for some protected species but there is a generous daily 'bag' limit. Phil Anthony (tel: (407) 281–0845) is a fishing guide of 12-years standing who promises clients that they will catch 'a trophy'. General Florida fishing information is available from Florida Game and Fresh Water Fish Commission, 3900 Drane Field Road, Lakeland FL 33811 (tel: (813) 648–3202).

With abundant catches, saltwater

Gone fishing; on the St John's

anglers are often content to fish from the seashore for blackfin tuna, flatfish and dolphin (not Flipper's mammalian cousins but a fish species of the same name). Real adventurers go big-game fishing for blue marlin, swordfish, barracuda and shark.

GOLF
Orlando is a golfing holiday destination par excellence. Walt Disney World alone has five superb championship courses. They are very busy and very expensive, however. For tee-times call the central booking number (407) 824–2270.

There are several other good golf clubs in the immediate Orlando area: Cypress Creek Country Club, Orlando, tel: (407) 351–2187; Hunter's Creek, Orlando, tel: (407) 240–4653; Marriot Orlando World Center, Orlando, tel: (407) 239–4200; MetroWest Country Club, Orlando, tel: (407) 299–1099; Orange Lake Country Club, Kissimmee, tel: (407) 239–0000; Poinciana Golf and Racquet Resort, Poinciana (near Kissimmee), tel: (407) 933–5300; Timucuan Golf and Country Club, Lake Mary, near Orlando, tel: (407) 321–0010; and Wedgefield Golf and Country Club, Orlando, tel: (407) 568–2116.

HORSE RIDING
Novices, from nine upwards, can ride gentle steeds at Disney's Fort Wilderness (tel: (407) 824–2803). Kissimmee's Poinciana Riding Stables (tel: (407)

Making your own waves is much more fun than just watching!

847–4343) has gentle and more adventurous trekking rides along old logging trails.

TENNIS

Walt Disney World has a number of courts for hire. The largest number are to be found at the Contemporary Resort (tel: (407) 824–3578) and the Dolphin and the Swan hotels shared courts (tel: (407) 934–4396). Next door to Disney is the Orange Lake Country Club, where the 16 courts are cheap and reservations are not necessary (tel: (407) 239–0000). Lake Cane Tennis Center on Turkey Lake Road, Orlando (tel: (407) 352–4913) is another good budget option, while the Orlando Tennis Center, located on West Livingstone Street, downtown, has good facilities and 16 courts (tel: (407) 246–2162).

WATERSPORTS

Waterskiing is available within Disney on Bay Lake (tel: (407) 824–2621). Just outside Disney, the Orange Country Club also offers jet skis and jet boats plus more sedate paddleboats and canoes for hire (tel: (407) 239–4444). An alternative is Splash 'n' Ski, based at Sand Lake, southwest of Orlando. Jet skis and windsurfers are also available here (tel: (407) 352–1494).

YACHTING

There are a number of marinas located within Walt Disney World which hire out wind- and motor-powered craft. Children will enjoy the small motorised 'water-sprite' boats available from the Disney Village Marketplace Marina, but they have a rather tame top speed for adult pilots.

Eating Out

*W*ith thousands of restaurants to choose from, eating out is a passion in Orlando. Quantity often gets the better of quality but at least the fierce competition usually means prices are low by European standards. *Orlando's Best*, available from hotel desks, gives comprehensive restaurant listings.

The first treat of the day!

Breakfast

The traditional American breakfast starts the day with such options as maple syrup pancakes, streaky bacon (done to a crisp), hash browns, English muffins, scrambled eggs (sometimes with peppers), raisin pumpernickel toast and as much coffee as you can drink. This is when hotel restaurants are at their busiest, the best of them offering expansive buffet selections at reasonable cost.

Lunch

Holidaymakers often take lunch on the hoof, choosing from such street-food staples as hamburgers, French fries, fried chicken and pizzas. A light lunch of fresh Florida seafood, or grilled fish with salad, makes a pleasant and healthier alternative.

Dinner

Sundown is the time to start thinking about serious eating and drinking and dinner is usually taken at around 6.30pm to 7pm.

Steaks, dependably huge, juicy and full of flavour, succulent ribs and pot roasts will satisfy the heartiest of appetites, while the choice of ethnic food on offer matches that of most major cities. Note that vegetables are rarely on offer. 'Fries' (chips) or 'jacket' (baked) potatoes with a salad are standard accompaniments to most meals.

Desserts are usually oversize, over-elaborate and well over the calorie count, but holidaymakers still drool over Mississippi Mud Pie, Pecan Pie, Death

ETIQUETTE

When it says on the menu that the main course (*entrée*) comes with salad be aware that the salad will be brought to you separately before the rest of the main course, unless you request otherwise.

Portions are almost universally huge. Sharing desserts is quite common and even sharing starters is acceptable. Asking for a 'doggy bag' is also an accepted practice and indeed in some restaurants seems to be the norm.

Tipping is almost obligatory. Waiting staff rely on gratuities for most of their wage and if you don't leave the customary 15 per cent they will let you know in no uncertain terms. On the positive side this usually means service is good, if sometimes rather obsequious. However if it is sub-standard, or the bare minimum, stand your ground and do not tip.

alcohol-free beers. American adults however, are not phased at the idea of asking for a soft drink to accompany their meal. Non-alcoholic fruit cocktails can be superb, while children love the delicious milk shakes and soda floats.

Sunday brunch

Sundays are made special by the American tradition of the huge Sunday brunch (breakfast and lunch in one). This is served buffet-style and the best ones include champagne and fresh orange juice to make up Buck's Fizz.

Theme park eating

Queues for lunch can be as horrendous as those for the rides – and at busy times it is vital to pre-book as soon as you arrive at the park. It also pays to take meals earlier or later than normal. Standards of food at the parks vary enormously. The restaurants at Epcot's World Showcase are deservedly acclaimed and the food at Splendid China is also very highly recommended.

by Chocolate, Mom's Deep Crust Apple Pie and other American specialities. And American ice cream is quite simply the best. Unfortunately coffee is universally weak and often poor quality – for most Europeans constant refills at no extra charge is a dubious benefit!

Alcoholic drinks are reasonably priced by European standards. Most bars feature a wide range from around the world, as well as American beers like Bud, Schlitz and Coors and the wines of California and Washington State.

Drink-driving laws are strict and this has led to a profusion of low-alcohol and

A typical welcoming restaurant sign on International Drive

Where to Eat

*L*isting all of Orlando's eating places would demand a book in itself. Below is a judicious selection of the best, drawn from across the price scale. The price coding indicates average prices to expect for a meal, including coffee but exclusive of drinks and tips.

$ Inexpensive – $10 or below
$$ Moderate – $10-$15
$$$ Expensive – $16-$25
$$$$ Exclusive – over $25 and upwards

AMERICAN

Dux ($$$$)

Consistently rated in Florida's top 10, The Dux is the principle restaurant at the plush Peabody Orlando Hotel, serving a mix of modern American and classic Continental cuisines. The hotel also boasts the excellent Capriccio Trattoria ($$$) and Beeline Diner ($$), a brilliant reproduction of a classic 1950s American diner, where the spirit of *The Last Picture Show* lives on and the breakfasts are awesome.
Peabody Hotel, 9801 International Drive, Orlando. Tel: (407) 352–4000. Jacket required in Dux.

Bubble Room ($$$)

They don't come much more eccentric than this wacky establishment just north of Winter Park. The décor comprises

eye-catching show-biz and entertainment industry *memorabilia* from the 1930s, '40s and '50s. Toy trains, twinkling coloured lights and more than 2,000 movie-stills fill every nook and cranny of this labyrinthine venue, with big band music pounding from vintage juke boxes. Servers ('Bubble Scouts') wear khaki shirts covered with buttons and pins, scarves with woggles, shorts and comical hats. Have a good look round before settling down to the gargantuan portions. The star dish is a 32-ounce 'prime-rib Weismuller' steak, acclaimed 'the best in the States' on the *Today* television show. Kids' dishes come in what could pass for adult portions elsewhere.
1351 South Orlando Avenue (Highway 17–92), Maitland. Tel: (407) 628–3331.

Hard Rock Café ($$)

The world-famous chain that started in London back in 1971, is now on the Orlando scene, housed in a guitar-shaped building at the gateway to Universal Studios. There's a priceless collection of rock 'n' roll *memorabilia* of more than 500 individual items, including Elvis Presley's Gibson acoustic guitar, the trademark collarless suits worn by the Beatles on their first US tour in 1964, a Fender guitar autographed by Eric Clapton, Jan and Dean's autographed 1967 surfboard and items from Bob Dylan, U2, David Bowie, Buddy Holly and even the Sex Pistols.

Hard Rock Café – the burger kings

The Bubble Room – great tasting food with a strange taste in décor!

Food is solidly American, including burgers, barbecue hickory-smoked chicken, the house Pig Sandwich special and New York Strip (sirloin) steak. *Universal Studios, Orlando. Tel: (407) 351–7625. No reservations (often long queues).*

Park Plaza Gardens ($$$$)

Resident Irish chef Tony Reilly spent four years at London's Fifty One-Fifty One before working with cajun-style cuisine in New Orleans. His present eclectic mix of flavours also tips its hat to the Florida Key's Caribbean-influenced cuisine and oriental tastes. It's now very much the place to be seen, and, thanks to its indoor trees and glass roof, a summery spot even in winter. Park Plaza Gardens offers such delights as poached red snapper in grapefruit, vodka and cream sauce and piquant crispy roast duck. Sauces and garnishes are never allowed to swamp the natural flavours. *319 Park Avenue, Winter Park. Tel: (407) 645–2475.*

Pebbles ($$-$$$)

A full menu of well presented fish, seafood and meat specialities is available throughout the day. The ambience suits both the casual and the formally dressed guest. Families are welcome. *17 West Church Street, Orlando (tel: (407) 839–0892); Crossroads, Lake Buena Vista (tel: (407) 827–1111); 2516 Aloma Avenue, Winter Park (tel: (407) 678–7001); 2110 West State Road 434, Longwood (tel: (407) 774–7111). No reservations.*

BARBECUE

Damon's – The Place For Ribs ($$)

Lean, meaty ribs, covered with Damon's hallmark barbecue sauce are the house speciality. Damon's is also renowned for its aged beefsteaks and a succulent loaf of onion rings. Go armed with a suitably large appetite!

Mercado Mediterranean Village, 8445 South International Drive, Orlando. Tel: (407) 352–5984.

Bob Evans Restaurant and Country Store ($)

Sample 'Good food in the American tradition' – featuring freshly prepared hickory-smoked chicken, steak, ribs and tasty fish.

6014 Canadian Court, International Drive (north of Bee-Line Expressway), Orlando. Tel: (407) 352–2161.

Orlando features good Chinese cooking

CHINESE

Ming Court ($$$)

This stylish 400-seat gourmet restaurant features innovative Oriental cuisine from the four corners of China, as well as fresh Florida seafood, marinaded steaks and grills. A light, airy and relaxing atmosphere is enhanced by picture windows overlooking flowering gardens, oriental fish ponds and waterfalls. Freshly prepared Cantonese-style dim sum is served daily.

9188 International Drive, Orlando. Tel: (407) 351–9988.

Peacock Paradise ($$)

The combination dinners for two here are highly recommended. Great lobster and crabmeat specialities.

6129 Westwood Boulevard, Orlando. Tel: (407) 363–0103.

Sum Chow's ($$$)

Butterflied giant shrimp in garlic sauce, curry-dusted lobster tail, and duck in sweet and sour bean sauce are among the house specialities at this contemporary Chinese restaurant.

Walt Disney World Dolphin Hotel, Lake Buena Vista. Tel: (407) 934–4000.

ENGLISH

The Windsor Tea Room ($)

Traditional Cornish pasties, Scotch egg and ploughman's lunches win praise from locals and holidaymakers at this suburban location.

114 West 4th Avenue, Mount Dora. Tel: (904) 735–2551.

ITALIAN

Christini's Ristorante Italiano ($$$)

Ivy Award-winner Chris Christini has a formidable international record stretching back 36 years, which includes stints at New York's 21 Club, the Four Seasons, and Epcot's Alfredo's di Roma. Bringing a personal touch to a menu rooted in classical Italian cuisine, his star items include fettuccini alla Christini and an incredible 36-ounce veal chop.

The Marketplace, Dr Phillips Boulevard/ Sand Lake Road, Orlando. Tel: (407) 345–8770.

Luciano's ($$)

The chef's specialities include a wickedly indulgent gnocchi (pasta dumplings) in aurora sauce, flavoured with garlic and basil; seafood ravioli; veal stuffed with cheese and ham; and traditional pastas, including angel hair with bacon, onions and olives.

2149 South Hiawassee Road, MetroWest Village, Southwest Orlando. Tel: (407) 292–9228.

Pacino's ($$)

A modern trattoria with a great line in pastas plus chicken, seafood and meats. Especially recommended is the mouth-watering fruits of the sea featuring ocean-fresh lobster, shrimp, calamari and mussels cooked in garlic, white wine and marinara.

5795 West Highway 192, Kissimmee. Tel: (407) 239–1141.

JAPANESE
Benihana ($$$)

Rocky Aoki adapted Japanese cooking to American tastes back in the 1960s and today his chain operates worldwide. Nimble-fingered chefs grill the food right at your table in this smart and highly popular branch.

Hilton Hotel, 1751 Hotel Plaza Boulevard, Lake Buena Vista. Tel: (407) 827–4865.

Kobe ($$)

Steak, chicken and seafood are prepared before your eyes in spectacular fashion on the teppanyaki table. It's not just a meal – it's a floor show!

2901 Parkway Boulevard (I–4, exit 25a), Kissimmee (tel: (407) 396–8088); 8460 Palm Parkway, Vista Center (I–4, exit 27), Lake Buena Vista (tel: (407) 239–1119); 468 West Highway 436 (I–4, exit 48W), Altamont Springs (tel: (407) 862–2888); 2110 East Colonial Drive (I–4, exit 41), Orlando (tel: (407) 895–6868).

MEXICAN
Paco's ($$)

Eternally crowded, thanks to great Tex-Mex food at easy-on-the-pocket prices. Tacos, burritos, nachos, refried beans and all the usual favourites are here. Surroundings are bright, portions are huge and there are some good beers to wash it all down.

1801 West Fairbanks Avenue, Winter Park. Tel: (407) 629–0149.

Italian food with a touch of opera

THE FLORIDA FLAVOUR

Surrounded as it is by sea and with countless lakes and waterways, it is no surprise that the mainstay of Florida cooking is fish and shellfish. In Central Florida you can sample the full range: from the conch (pronounced 'conk' – it's a delicate-flavoured mollusc) of the Keys, to the catfish associated with the north of the state and 'po' boy' ('poor boy') Southern cooking. Fish you won't find at home include scrod, yellowtail, pompano and dolphin (don't worry, the latter is a fish, not the friendly mammal). They are all good. So too, are Maine lobster, crawfish ('Florida lobster') and various types of crab. Stone crabs are a speciality of Southern Florida and only the claws are eaten (the crab is thrown back into the sea to grow another claw!).

In America of course steak is always on the menu and is consistently good. A New York Strip is sirloin while a prime-rib steak is very similar to British roast beef.

Cajun, or creole-style cooking comes from Louisiana and is very popular in Florida. Typical dishes are blackened grouper or blackened meats. The blackening comes from the spices, not proximity to the grill, so don't be put off – this is some of America's tastiest cooking. Jambalaya is a kind of Cajun paella. The other main ethnic food that you probably won't be familiar with is Cuban which is very popular in Southern Florida, due to the large immigrant population there. This is very much Spanish-style cooking, often with a tropical twist, as typified by the national dish, chicken with rice (arroz con pollo) served with plantains (a tropical banana-like fruit).

Remnants of the old-style native Florida 'Cracker Cooking' include breakfast items such as grits (boiled ground corn) and biscuits and gravy.

The latter is a strange mixture of savoury scones and a white-sauce flavoured with meat (you may see chicken and biscuit on sale as a lunch snack). Later in the day you may get to try hush puppies (deep-fried corn meal dough), catfish and even alligator tail. The latter tastes a little like chicken but, with the best will in the world, none of

these 'Cracker' foods are likely to set your taste buds alight. Like most native Florida food, it's pleasant but it tends to be bland.

To end your meal there is (often literally) just one Florida dessert, the famous Key Lime pie. This is a cousin of lemon meringue pie and is made with limes from the Florida Keys and condensed milk. However, it usually lacks the sharp tang of a good lemon meringue pie and is likely to be too sweet for many visitors.

Meat-eaters will have a mouth-watering time in Florida

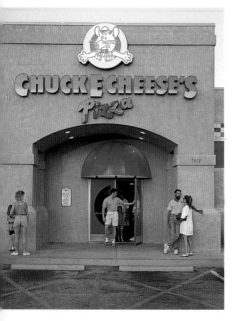

A ubiquitous cheap 'n' cheerful Orlando pizza parlour

crab legs, baked stuffed clams, oysters Rockefeller, steamed little-neck clams, peel-and-eat shrimps and lots more besides (including delicious ribs for those who aren't into seafood).
3615 West Vine Street (US 192), Kissimmee (tel: (407) 932–1666); South Orange Blossom Trail, at Sand Lake Road, Orlando (tel: (407) 438–0607).

Charlie's Lobster House ($$$)
Live Maine lobsters, anyway you like them, fried Florida alligator (it's a little like chicken), stuffed whole flounder and Maryland crab cakes (made with lump crabmeat and red and green peppers), are among the favourites at this spot.
Mercado Mediterannean Village, 8445 South International Drive, Orlando. Tel: (407) 352–6929.

The Crab House ($$$)
These two seafood speciality houses are renowned for their seafood buffet bar, featuring freshly shucked oysters and clams on the half shell, cold steamed shrimp, mussels, crab, fresh vegetables and salads – make as many visits as you like. There's also a changing menu of fresh fish, with grouper, mahi-mahi, snapper, tuna, swordfish and other species appearing according to season.
8496 Palm Parkway, Vista Center Shoppes, Lake Buena Vista (tel: (407) 239–1888); 8291 International Drive, Goodings Plaza, Orlando (tel: (407) 352–6140).

Gary's Duck Inn ($$)
Nautical décor and seafood menu, which includes fresh snapper and crab.
3974 S Blossom Trail, Orlando. Tel: (407) 843–0270.

The Ocean Grill ($$)
Fried clams, catfish, swordfish and a range of surf 'n' turf items are featured

PIZZA
Donato's ($)
Award-winning New York-style pizzas plus pastas, renowned salads and giant 'subs' (huge French loaf sandwiches). There is also an authentic Italian deli counter here.
5159 International Drive, Orlando, close by the Belz Factory Outlet. Tel: (407) 363–5959.

Johnny's Pizza Palace ($)
Pizzas of every description, pasta and generous sandwiches.
4909 Lake Underhill Road, Orlando. Tel: (407) 277–3452.

SEAFOOD
Boston Lobster Feast ($$$)
Great value, all-you-can-eat seafood feasts are the speciality of these twin restaurants. Maine lobster, Alaskan snow

here. Try the 8oz New York Strip (sirloin) steak served with a half pound of tasty Alaskan snow crab legs. Chicken in teriyaki sauce, topped with pineapple, and hickory-smoked baby back ribs keep non-fish eaters happy.
6432 International Drive, Orlando. Tel: (407) 352-9995.

STEAKS

Cattleranch ($)
Vast steaks sizzled over orange wood in a cowboy-style tourist-free zone.
6129 Old Winter Garden, Orlando. Tel: (407) 298-7334.

Outback ($$)
Luxuriant greenery, waiters in nifty bush suits; grilled steaks and seafood.
Buena Vista Palace Hotel, 1900 Buena Vista Drive, Buena Vista. Tel: (407) 827-3430.

Ponderosa Steak House ($)
Family restaurant, breakfast buffet, salad bar.
7598 W Irlo Bronson Memorial Highway, Kissimmee. Tel: (407) 396-7721. Also branches at 5771 W Irlo Bronson Memorial Highway (tel: (407) 397-2477); 6326/8510/14407 International Drive (tel: (407) 352-9343/354-1477/238-2526.

Ruth's Chris Steakhouse ($$-$$$)
Man-sized fillet steaks are the stars here – cooked to your preference.
Interior Decor Center, 999 Douglas Avenue (between Highways 434 and 436) Altamont Springs. Tel: (407) 682-644. Evenings only.

Western Steer ($)
Lunch sandwich specials here, including fries and a draft beer or soft beverage can cost less than $5. Western Steer is also renowned for its buffet breakfast, offering corn beef hash, biscuits and gravy, pork and beans, grits and other downhome specialities. Great value choice aged-beef steaks, too.
6315 International Drive (opposite Wet 'n' Wild), Orlando (tel: (407) 363-0677); Vista Center, 8594 Palm Parkway, Lake Buena Vista (tel: (407) 238-0496).

An elegant garden restaurant at Winter Park

FRUITS OF THE FIELD

Historians believe that it was the Spanish explorer, Ponce de León, who brought the first citrus fruits to Florida during his explorations in 1513. It is probable that as the Spaniards were searching around St Augustine for the Fountain of Youth, or simply gold, they dropped seeds from the Spanish fruits that they had brought with them.

The earliest groves developed around St Augustine and Tampa and the oldest continually cultivated orange grove in Florida is the Don Philippe grove, planted in Pinellas County by French aristocrat Odet Philippe during the early 1800s. By the early 1880s there were over 70 million citrus trees in the state. But its hasn't all been plain sailing; three times the groves have been devastated by frost –

in the late 1800s, in the early 1970s and latterly in the 1980s.

Today, Florida is the world's largest citrus-producing region and Orlando itself is ringed by thousands of acres of orange groves – a fact evident to any visitor who has taken a trip to the top of the Florida Citrus Tower in Clermont (see page 88).

Florida orange juice

Around a quarter of the world's commercially produced oranges and grapefruits and a massive 95 per cent of its limes are now produced in 'The Sunshine State' (accounting for 95

Florida. Surprisingly however, orange juice is no cheaper here than it is in Europe and if you stop at a farm shop, do be prepared to buy in large bagfuls.

per cent of the world's concentrate output). There are 8 main varieties of grapefruit and orange alone: March White grapefruit, red grapefruit, Duncan grapefruit (the best flavour), Valencia orange, Temple orange, Pineapple orange (acclaimed for its juicy sweetness), Navel orange and Hamelin orange. Visitors can enjoy the freshest fruits and juices at farm stalls, found beside the highways throughout Central

Hotels and Accommodation

*T*he standard of hotel accommodation in Orlando is high when compared to similar-price establishments in Europe, and there's usually lots of choice. Many overseas visitors are on a package holiday, with pre-booked accommodation. This can present the best value-for-money option, with the total price, sometimes including a hire car, coming to not much more than flight costs alone. But those visitors who like to keep on the move, or who prefer to see a hotel before committing themselves, should have no problem putting a roof over their head.

The Orlando Visitor Information Center, Mercado Mediterranean Village, International Drive, Orlando (tel: (407) 363–5876) offers a free hotels guide and can provide an up-to-the-minute vacancy list. Hotels are invariably well sign-posted, often displaying room rates

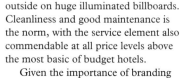

outside on huge illuminated billboards. Cleanliness and good maintenance is the norm, with the service element also commendable at all price levels above the most basic of budget hotels.

Given the importance of branding in the American market, the various chains strive hard for uniformity. Consequently, the type of star-rating system which is used in Europe has not been felt necessary.

At the top of the range are Hilton, Holiday Inn, Sheraton and Marriott while reliable mid-market names include Travelodge, Ramada, Radisson, Best Western, Quality Inn and Inns of America. In the budget sector, Days Inn and Howard Johnson offer reasonable standards.

Given the humid climate and the summertime presence of mosquitos and other bugs, rooms are invariably air-conditioned, with double-glazed sealed windows (specify a non-smoking room if lingering tobacco smells irritate). Large king-size beds are the norm, as are direct-dial telephones and big-screen TV sets. Suites often offer a fully-equipped kitchen. Mini-bars, trouser presses and hairdriers are far

Many of Orlando's hotels are sleek, modern and high rise

Every good hotel has its own swimming pool

less common, and baths – if they are provided – tend to be impracticably small and cramped, since most Americans prefer an invigorating shower to a relaxed soak.

While a number of properties have their gimmicks, most Orlando hotels are faceless, multi-floored, 300–1,000 room architectural nonentities offering fairly standardised facilities.

Unlike in Europe, hotel restaurants usually compete on price with restaurants on the street and are increasingly franchised.

Across the board, room prices are considerably lower than at equivalent European hotels and prices are quoted for the room, rather than the number of guests. This can mean real bargains for large families who are prepared to share the same room. Breakfast is rarely, if ever, included in the room price.

WHERE TO STAY

Most Orlando hotels are mere bed factories devoid of any character or individuality, guests make their choice based solely on price and convenience of location. However, spearheaded by the imaginatively themed properties within the Walt Disney World Village, there is a trend towards providing more of a home-from-home environment and 'suite hotels', which allow guests to cook in their own kitchen, are becoming increasingly popular.

Rather than driving to the coast, most visitors are happy to laze around a hotel pool and the better hotels provide welcoming poolside bars and dining.

Some establishments offer a shuttle bus service to the major attractions and secure parking is available at luxury hotels for a small fee.

STAYING WITH MICKEY

At his original Disneyland, in California, Walt Disney made the mistake of thinking his business would be built on day-trippers. Consequently, other entrepreneurs snapped up surrounding land and scooped most of the huge volume of hotel business his theme park generated. No such error was made at Walt Disney World, where 20 huge Disney associate hotels – several operating as virtually self-contained resorts – are located within the Walt Disney World Village complex and on nearby Hotel Plaza. These premises are leased to some of the world's most respected hotel organisations and are operated to meticulous standards defined by the Disney corporation, which owns the land they sit on.

Hotel Plaza, close to the Village, offers good quality ordinary-style establishments. However, hotels within the main Disney complex are themed. The clapboard-clad Beach Club, for instance, re-creates New England while

The classy Disney's Yacht Club Resort

the Polynesian facility features longhouse-style accommodation blocks.

But does staying within Walt Disney World represent good value? The only major advantage of being a Disney guest is proximity to the parks. This is not as crass as it sounds. For it means you can go from the parks back to your own hotel as often as you wish within the day. When opening hours are extended this is a real advantage. Even visitors from Kissimmee, a mere stone's throw away, will think twice about making that long trudge back to the car park.

Think too about how much more of Orlando you want to see. If you are happy to visit the Disney parks almost exclusively – and there is an awful lot to see – then you may be able to save the extra dollars that you pay over and above a comparable Orlando hotel on car hire.

If you are on a tight budget but you are still determined to be 'an insider', consider the Fort Wilderness resort where the atmosphere is relaxed and friendly and a tent or RV (recreational vehicle/camper van) site is perhaps the best value for money in Disney World.

Luxury hotels

Orlando's top hotels are among the best in the world – and have prices to match (around $250 a night for the best rooms). Polished marble, gleaming brass and acres of smoked glass are *de rigeur*.

Mid-price

Most of Orlando's major hotel chains come in to this category and combine the convenience of the most up-to-date facilities with the leisure and recreation amenities expected of a resort-hotel, ie including sports facilities and a choice of shops and restaurants.

Budget

Motels (cheap hotels on main highways) remain an American institution and Orlando offers a huge range of convenient 'drive-in' properties at often surprisingly low rates.

Many of the cheaper hotels are located around the Orange Blossom Trail (Route 441). As a tourist trap, parts of this district are both noisy and less than salubrious. It's better to drive to a suburban location like Lake Buena Vista, Crossroads or Kissimmee for such low-cost accommodation.

Suites

Suites, or lodges, offer the convenience of an apartment of your own, allied to full hotel facilities, rather like a European aparthotel. This is an increasingly popular option with families who want that bit more space and the option to cook their own meals when desired.

Bed and breakfast

Not to be confused with the small, cheap and cheerful British-style B&B, the American offering is an expensive personalised inn, small by American

The post-modern WDW Dolphin

standards, usually with less than 30 rooms. Orlando has a small number of these but they are generally to be found in leafy suburban areas or out in the country, far away from the neon of International Drive. They are certainly not the cheapest accommodation but arguably they are the most amenable.

Youth hostels

Orlando's one and only hostel is a pretty Spanish-style building (Orlando Plantation Manor, 227 N Eola Drive, Orlando, (tel: (407) 843–8888) overlooking picturesque Lake Eola. There is also a youth hostel at St Augustine at 32 Treasury Street (tel: (904) 829–6163).

Resort homes

For roughly the same price as a hotel room, visitors can rent fully furnished condominiums (apartments) and vacation homes. Write to the Orlando Information Center (see page 168) for a list of letting agencies.

Orlando on a Budget

*T*he theme parks of Orlando offer good value for money, with a single ticket providing a full day's entertainment. For a family, however, they are undeniably expensive. An Orlando holiday will never be cheap but with a little planning and a little 'inside information' it can be a lot less expensive.

The easiest way to save money is to pick up discount coupons. These are available at your hotel, from tourist information points, in local newspapers, freesheets – in fact just about everywhere. Armed with these coupons it is quite feasible to spend a whole fortnight in Orlando without paying the stated price at your accommodation, at any attraction (except Walt Disney World – see opposite) or at any restaurant.

Make your first stop the Orlando Visitor Center located at the Mercado Mediterranean Village on International Drive. Here you can pick up, free of charge, the Orlando Magicard which is effectively a coupon booklet in credit card format. This offers 10 to 50 per cent savings at well over 100 outlets including hotels, restaurants, car rentals and shops. It is only possible to get a card by calling in person or telephoning within Florida (tel: (800) 551–0180). Before you book accommodation, write

to the Kissimmee-St Cloud Convention and Visitors Bureau (see page 189) and they will send you a brochure including special accommodation discount coupons.

ATTRACTIONS

There are very few cheap or free worthwhile attractions in Central Florida; the shining exception is Kennedy Space Center Spaceport USA (see page 100). Holidaymakers in search of nature will find Florida's natural parks are a lot easier on the pocket than the theme parks. Water parks offer reduced price admission in the late afternoon, which is worth taking up if opening hours are extended. Golf courses also offer cheap rates after a certain time.

Busch Entertainment Corporation offer discount packages if you visit all of their attractions, ie Cypress Gardens, Sea World and Busch Gardens. Enquire at any one of these.

EATING OUT

If you're willing to sacrifice quality for quantity, simply look on the huge billboards, especially along International Drive. Breakfasts and 'early-bird' evening specials can provide excellent value for money. Eat well at breakfast so that you don't have to eat at the theme parks. As a rule theme-park food is mediocre and overpriced. You're not supposed to take your own food or drink into any theme park but a surreptitious sandwich shouldn't go amiss.

When it comes to dinner, American portions are often huge so don't worry about a starter.

CAR HIRE

Costs vary widely and you may well end up comparing apples and pears. CDW (Collision Damage Waiver) insurance, which you can only buy from the car-hire company (or their agent) is absolutely essential. However, when it comes to personal and belongings insurance, beware of high pressure sales patter from desk clerks persuading you to take their insurance in addition to any policy you already have.

If you are travelling from the UK, Holiday Autos, Europe's largest car rental brokers, guarantee lowest hire prices and always use reputable local companies, tel: (0171) 491–1111.

SEASONALITY

Visiting Orlando out of high season can make a big difference to your accommodation. If you are travelling independently don't be afraid to ask a hotel what their very best rate is.

SHOPPING

There are a few real bargains to be had in Orlando so don't be fooled by all the marketing razzamatazz. Try discount outlets like Belz or Flea World (see pages 134–5), but choose well.

WALT DISNEY WORLD

Not for nothing is it sometimes called 'Wallet Disney World'. Aside from reduced price admission to the water parks (see above) there are no bargians on offer here. If you see a booth offering discount Walt Disney World tickets there is a catch, usually involving high-pressure time-share salesmen.

On Business

*B*usiness in Orlando usually means tourism, but over the last decade the city and Central Florida in general have attracted more than their share of new businesses outside the tourism sphere. Indeed, the influential *Fortune* magazine recently listed Orlando as among America's top 20 cities for business opportunity. With Florida as the fastest growing large state in the country, there is a huge ready-made 'home market' plus international markets. Manufacturing, agriculture and high technology activities all contribute to the region's dynamic economy. And of course there are countless professional (and some not-so-professional) services riding on the back of both tourism and the new industries.

Florida has undergone many boom and bust periods and to an extent is still frontier country: land costs are relatively low, labour rates are competitive, corporation income tax is a mere 5.5 per cent and other taxes are negligible. In fact Florida is claimed to be the cheapest place to do business in the US.

Metro Orlando, the economic development commission of Central Florida, helps smooth international trade and can offer practical advice and contacts. Write to them at 200 East Robinson Street, Suite 600, Orlando FLA 32801 (tel: (407) 422–7159). The Florida Division of Economic Development deals with state-wide business development: The Collins building, Tallahassee, Florida 32301. Tel: (904) 488–5507.

ACCOMMODATION

Greater Orlando makes life simple for visiting business people with a wealth of hotels and motels conveniently sited on major routes, offering all business services at very reasonable prices.

COMMUNICATIONS

With its major international airport and location at the hub of Florida's road network Orlando is well placed for business within the state and overseas.

CONFERENCES

Florida is a popular business destination, both for serious conferences and corporate entertainment, so has good experience of catering for both organisers and delegates. Here in the land of communications and marketing you'll never be short of the tools for the job, nor any number of willing ground service suppliers and advisers to help you. As for entertainment after hours and during time off, it would be difficult to find a better place in the world – as long as your delegates are young at heart.

Most large hotels have good conference facilities. If you want to put your conference in the hands of one of the world's most successful communications corporations and enjoy the best possible hospitality facilities contact Walt Disney Village (tel: (407) 828–3200).

A brand new facility located near Disney Village Marketplace offers banqueting and meetings for groups of up to 500 people. Corporate and incentive business is an area into which Disney is currently rapidly expanding.

Two other options for large-scale conferences and exhibitions (as well as smaller conferences and seminars) are Church Street Station (see pages 144–5) and the Orange County Convention and Civic Center on International Drive (tel: (407) 345–9800). Both have extensive facilities, though for glamour, the Georgian Private Parlour Rooms at Church Street are hard to beat.

ETIQUETTE

Most Americans are outgoing and informal, very quickly on to first name terms and eager to please with hospitality which is as much an extension of their character as a business convention. Behind a naïve exterior may well be a very shrewd commercial brain so never underestimate the New World way of business.

Don't forget, in the USA presentation and packaging is vital, so professionally prepared sales literature, good quality photographs, plans, video presentations and the like are very necessary.

The thrusting new downtown face of Orlando

Practical Guide

ARRIVING

Passports

EU citizens visiting for less than 90 days do not require a visa. They must, however, be in possession of a current full passport (a visitor's passport is not sufficient). Failure to carry the proper documentation will cause enormous problems on arrival – if you get that far, since airlines now carry out stringent passport examinations before issuing boarding passes. Check with your travel agent or the nearest US Embassy, consulate or tourism office before you leave if you are in doubt over visa requirements.

Visa waiver forms are handed out during the flight, along with customs declarations. These must be completed and handed in at immigration control on arrival. Your declaration form should list anything you are bringing into the US – whether an intended gift, sample or the like – which is not for your own personal use. There is no limit to the amount of US or foreign currency which may be taken in and out, though large amounts must be declared. If in doubt, ask – penalties can be punitive.

By air

More than two dozen air carriers operate scheduled services to Orlando. There are also numerous charter flights run by tour operators – Virgin, Delta, United and Northwest are among the busiest airlines. It pays to shop around for special deals and discounts. Lower fares can sometimes be obtained by taking non-direct flights via such major air-network hubs as Amsterdam, Paris, London, New York and Miami.

Most domestic and international passengers will arrive at Orlando International Airport. The main concourse is spacious and decidedly user-friendly, with top quality shopping

Interstate 4: this usually busy highway is used by virtually every visitor

and refreshments outlets.

Various regular bus services link the airport with Lake Buena Vista, International Drive and Downtown Orlando hotels (Airport Transfer, tel: (407) 422–0744). Taxis are inexpensive by European standards.

By bus

Orlando is on Greyhound Lines national network while Gray Lines (tel: (437) 422–0744) serves the airport, the major hotels and attractions. Lynx Tri-County Transit (tel: (437) 841–8241) provides a local bus service across the metropolis.

By car

Major highway routes serving Orlando include: Interstate 75 (I–75) from the midwest, connecting with the Florida Turnpike, which continues down to Miami; Interstate 95 (I–95) from the Atlantic coast states; and Interstate 4 (I–4) which runs east/west through Orlando and connects with Daytona and Tampa.

By train

AmTrak services connect Orlando directly with Miami, Tampa and New York, with stops in Winter Park and Sanford. Sleeper services are available. Contact National Railroad Passenger Corporation (tel: (305) 835–1202) or (Amtrak (800) 872–7245) for schedules and prices. A Florida Regional Railpass offers savings for multi-journeys.

The *Thomas Cook Overseas Timetable*, which is published bi-monthly and gives details of many rail, bus and shipping services worldwide, will help you plan a rail journey around the US. It is available in the UK from some stations, any branch of Thomas Cook or by phoning (01733) 268943. In the US contact the Forsyth Travel Library Inc, 9154 West 57th St (PO Box 2975), Shawnee Mission, Kansas 66201 (tel:(800) 367–7892 – toll free).

CAMPING

There is plenty of opportunity in and around Orlando for camping, whether in

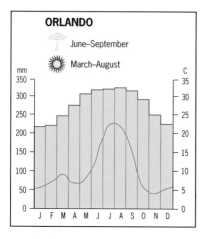

ORLANDO

June–September

March–August

a tent, an RV (Recreational Vehicle) or static trailer home. Walt Disney World devotes the huge 650-acre Fort Wilderness resort to camping, offering over 800 wooded sites for tents, RVs and luxuriously kitted trailers with air-conditioning and TVs. Alternatives include the popular Yogi Bear's Jellystone Park, Fort Summit's Western-style campground at Baseball City (I–4/US27 interchange) and the lakeside Port O' Call Campground in Kissimmee. All these are large, with the sort of facilities that obviate any pressing need to experience nature at first hand. Simpler, more backwoodsy options can be found in the attractive Wekiwa River area north of Orlando (log cabins to rent) or in Lakeland to the west.

The *Florida Camping Directory*, an annual publication, is available free from Florida Campground Association, Department D-8, 1638 North Plaza Drive, Tallahassee, FL 32308–5323 (tel: (904) 656–8878). The American Automobile Association (AAA) also produces a list of camping grounds.

CHILDREN

There has never been a holiday destination which has geared itself more towards children. Besides all the child-orientated attractions, hotels and restaurants provide a warm welcome to families and facilities like highchairs and baby-change rooms are the norm.

Remember, though, that taking in all the sights can prove very tiring for children and they also need protecting from too much sunshine.

CLIMATE

See climate chart.

CONSULATES

Australia: 636 Fifth Avenue, New York NY. Tel: (212) 245–4000.
Canada: 1251 Avenue of the Americas, New York NY. Tel: (212) 586–2400.
Republic of Ireland: 515 Madison Avenue, New York NY. Tel: (212) 319–2555.
UK: 1001 South Bayshore Drive, Suite 2110, Miami FL.. Tel: (305) 374–1522.

CONVERSION TABLES

See opposite.

CUSTOMS REGULATIONS

Hand your customs declaration form to Customs. It should list all things brought into the US, whether gifts for others or not. There is no limit to the amount of cash or travellers' cheques you may bring in or take out. Prohibited items include fresh meat, fruit, drugs (other than prescribed) and plants. Regulations are currently under review – check before leaving. Duty-free allowances for travellers aged over 21: 200 cigarettes and 100 cigars and 1 litre of spirits. Travellers aged 18–21: no spirits allowed (check for changes).

Conversion Table

FROM	TO	MULTIPLY BY
Inches	Centimetres	2.54
Feet	Metres	0.3048
Yards	Metres	0.9144
Miles	Kilometres	1.6090
Acres	Hectares	0.4047
Gallons	Litres	4.5460
Ounces	Grams	28.35
Pounds	Grams	453.6
Pounds	Kilograms	0.4536
Tons	Tonnes	1.0160

To convert back, for example from centimetres to inches, divide by the number in the the third column.

Men's Suits

UK		36	38	40	42	44	46	48
Rest of Europe	46	48	50	52	54	56	58	
US		36	38	40	42	44	46	48

Dress Sizes

UK		8	10	12	14	16	18
France		36	38	40	42	44	46
Italy		38	40	42	44	46	48
Rest of Europe		34	36	38	40	42	44
US		6	8	10	12	14	16

Men's Shirts

UK	14	14.5	15	15.5	16	16.5	17
Rest of Europe	36	37	38	39/40	41	42	43
US	14	14.5	15	15.5	16	16.5	17

Men's Shoes

UK	7	7.5	8.5	9.5	10.5	11
Rest of Europe	41	42	43	44	45	46
US	8	8.5	9.5	10.5	11.5	12

Women's Shoes

UK	4.5	5	5.5	6	6.5	7
Rest of Europe	38	38	39	39	40	41
US	6	6.5	7	7.5	8	8.5

DISABLED TRAVELLERS

You will invariably find ramps, wide doors, lifts and other wheelchair provisions in resort hotels, larger restaurants, theme parks and other popular areas. Some hotels have telephones specially designed for hearing-impaired people.

Disabled people are officially referred to as being 'physically challenged'. *The Physically Challenged Guide to Florida* is a comprehensive brochure, listing names, addresses and phone numbers of organisations that can help the disabled traveller. It is available from the Florida Department of Commerce, Division of Tourism, Visitor Enquiry, 107 West Gaines Street, Collins Building, Tallahassee, FL 32399–2000. Tel: (904) 488–7598.

DRIVING

Contact your car hire firm, either direct or through your travel agent for documentary proof of disabled driver status, such as the blue International

Car hire is cheap and easy, but remember to add on insurance

Access Symbol. When you arrive, the car rental company will point you to the local county office to claim status as a disabled visitor. The snag is that you may have to wait up to 2 hours for a disabled visitor badge which gives limited parking concessions. If you are using Orlando Airport, however, there is a helpful organisation which will speed your passage in this and many matters: Friends of the Family, Suite 209, The Entertainment Complex, 1727 Orlando Central Parkway, Orlando, FL 33809. Tel: (407) 856–7676. Fax: (407) 856–7516. Contact them in advance.

Car hire

European nationals can hire a car and drive in Florida on their own full driving licence, though an International Driving Permit may be useful. Would-be drivers aged under 25 may find hiring difficult or have to pay significantly more for travel insurance. Ask your travel agent about fly-drive schemes or booking before you leave home, as this may be cheaper than booking when in Florida. Take the booking form with you and present it to the car hire company (usually at or close to the airport). On top of this hire charge, you will be advised to take out Collision Damage Waiver (CDW) insurance. It is expensive – around $10-12 a day – but essential as it covers you for every tiny scratch to your hire car, which would otherwise be charged to you, irrespective of whose fault it was.

Almost all cars have automatic transmission, and all come with air-conditioning and an excellent stereo radio. Cars should be returned with a full tank of fuel (hire firms charge for top-ups at a far higher cost than you would obtain at a filling station).

Petrol (gas) is cheap (lead-free petrol is a little dearer). Some filling stations require you to pay before you fill up.

Roads and regulations

Americans drive on the right. If you feel nervous about driving on the right, it is worth making sure you arrive in daylight rather than tackle the first stretch in the dark. You will soon get used to it, but beware that you don't lose your concentration after stopping.

Types of road

The fastest routes around Florida are provided by the multi-lane Interstate freeways (equivalent to Britsih motorways). These are designated by an I, eg I–4. American drivers' lane discipline is poor, with overtaking on both sides a frequent occurrence. However, as traffic is only ever moving at a maximum of 65mph on wide clear roads, this isn't as alarming as it sounds.

Just remember to use your mirror frequently.

The next fastest roads are highways, which have a US designation, eg US–1. If you don't mind getting there a little more slowly look for a parallel, scenic route to the main highway, designated by an A suffix. State Routes are another form of highway, designated by the letters SR. County Roads (CR) are minor roads and should provide more atractive scenery than any of the above.

The most notable toll road is Florida's Turnpike, over 300 miles north to south. On some toll roads you get a distance marker when you go on and pay as you leave. On others, you pre-pay by throwing a selection of small coins into a basket. Tolls range from 25 cents to a few dollars. It is best to keep coins in the car, but don't panic if you don't have change, as attendants are always on hand. In towns, many roads have names as well as numbers, which sometimes change along their length.

Speed limits

The maximum speed limit is 65mph and on ordinary highways and busy freeway stretches this reduces to 55mph. In built-up areas, it is 30–35mph. If the police stop you, wait in the car and be polite. Be ready to produce your driving documents but do not start fumbling around. The officers may take this as a sign you are reaching for a gun. Humour won't help. Speeding offences sometimes go to court and a base fine is $54, plus $4 for every mile over the limit. Alternatively you may be fined on the spot.

Cities have good parking areas (often free) and parking meters costing from 25c to $1 an hour. Your wheels may be clamped for a parking offence, and a

sticker tells you where to pay the fine to obtain your car's release.

Drinking and driving

This is a serious offence and you can be locked up until you've taken a urine test, or lose your licence on the spot. The best advice is don't drink and drive. Any alcohol carried in a car must be unopened and be in the boot.

Highway breakdown

Emergency phones are situated only in official off-road parking areas. Wait with your vehicle, with the bonnet raised until the Highway Patrol stop to help you, otherwise call the All America helpline on 1–800–336–HELP.

If your hire car breaks down, phone the number on the dashboard sticker.

Chillin' out with a cool drink

Tongue-in-cheek souvenirs – pigging it on the beach

ELECTRICITY

The standard electricity supply is 110 (60 cycles). You may have to bring an adaptor to convert. Sockets take plugs with two flat pins. Appliances without dual voltage capability will also need a transformer. If in doubt ask at your hotel.

EMERGENCIES AND EMERGENCY PHONE NUMBERS

In an emergency, phone 911, then ask for the service you require.

Money

Most banks and issuers of travellers' cheques (and credit cards) give an emergency number to report thefts. Make sure you have a note of these (and cheque numbers) before you leave and keep them separately from your cheques. Report losses to the police,

and to these numbers:
Access/MasterCard: (1–800) 336–8472.
American Express Credit Cards: (1–800) 528–2121.
American Express Travellers' Cheques: (1–800) 221–7282.
Credit cards: (1–800) 528–2121. Diners Club card: (1–800) 968–8300.
Visa: (1–800) 627–6811 or (1–800) 227–6811.

The Thomas Cook Wordlwide Customer Promise offers free emergency assistance at any Thomas Cook Network location to travellers who have purchased their travel tickets through Thomas Cook. In addition, any MasterCard cardholder may use any Thomas Cook Network location to report loss or theft of their card and obtain an emergency card replacement, as a free service under the Thomas Cook MasterCard International Alliance. Thomas Cook

MasterCard Refund Centre: (24-hour service – report loss or theft within 24 hours): tel: (1)–800–223–7373 (toll-free).

Doctors, Dentists

Numbers are given in the Yellow Pages, under Dentists, Physicians and Surgeons, or Clinics, or phone the local casualty hospital.

HEALTH

There are no special inoculation requirements for visitors to Florida, which in spite of its sub-tropical climate is largely free of infectious diseases. Medical treatment is privatised and expensive. Doctor referral (tel: (407) 295–8280) and dentist referral (tel: 800–DENTIST) services will help you find rapid treatment. In case of emergency tel: 911.

There are plenty of 24-hour drug-stores offering branded pharmaceuticals.

Like every other part of the world, AIDS is present.

Florida's deceptively strong sunlight is waiting to catch out the foolhardy. Be sure to use a good quality sunscreen lotion – and don't forget you are at risk even when fully clothed, as the back of the neck and bald patches can soon burn and blister. A baseball cap or other sun hat is well worth having; so too is some insect repellant as, once you venture into the great outdoors, Florida is a paradise for creepy crawlies and biting insects.

Tap water is perfectly safe though overseas' visitors might find the highly chlorinated taste unpleasant.

INSURANCE

Medical costs are extremely high in the US. It is essential to take out full travel insurance for injury, illness, loss of luggage and other risks. Frequent travellers will find it far cheaper to take out an annual policy (individual policies for as few as three trips abroad will cost as much and offer fewer benefits).

LOST PROPERTY

Europeans are used to handing in lost property at police stations – and retrieving it in the same way. No such centralised system exists in the US. You must simply retrace your steps and make enquiries accordingly. If you left something on the plane, report it direct to the airline.

Report serious losses to the police or you will not be able to make an insurance claim.

T-shirts are reasonably priced and a very portable Florida souvenir

Orlando police are particularly helpful to visitors

starved of information, though most of it tends to be poor quality and extremely parochial. British newspapers are fairly easy to find, appearing one day after publication. The *Orlando Sentinel* gives daily coverage of what is happening and where, while various free 'what's on' magazines such as *TV & Visitors Guide* and *Travelhost* are usually to be found in hotel rooms.

MONEY MATTERS

America functions largely on plastic money, and Florida is no exception. Thomas Cook travellers' cheques should be carried in US dollars. These are accepted as cash in hotels, restaurants, gas stations and larger shops and change is given as appropriate without any extra commission being charged.

In practice you will therefore never need to change money at a bank.

Best accepted cards are MasterCard, American Express and Visa. Unless you have paid in advance you may be asked to show, or give an imprint of, your card as you check in at a hotel.

Almost everything will cost you six per cent more than you expect to pay as sales tax (similar to VAT) is not usually shown on ticket prices.

Thomas Cook desks, located in major hotels, make no service charge for Thomas Cook or MasterCard travellers' cheques and also offer a useful *Value Pak* booklet with various savings on purchases. Thomas Cook Guest Service Desks are at the following locations:

Fantasy Club Villas, 2935 Hart

MAPS

Good maps are vital, even once inside the theme parks. Tourist maps are widely available, free of charge, but tend to be lacking in detail. American road maps, like the road system itself, can be confusing until you adapt your mind to the local grid-system way of doing things. Buy the best map you can from home.

MEDIA

Round the clock 24-hour television, bulky newspapers and a profusion of magazines mean the Americans are never

Avenue, Kissimmee FL 34746. Tel:
(407) 396–1808).

Guest Quarters Resort, 2305 Hotel
Plaza Boulevard, Lake Buena Vista
FL32830. Tel: (407) 934–1000.

Holiday Inn, 6515 International Drive,
Orlando FL 32819. Tel: (407)
351–3500.

Holiday Inn, Maingate, 7300 West US
192, Kissimmee FL 34747. Tel: (407)
396–7300 or 239–7727.

Holiday Inn, across from Universal
Studios, Orlando.

Homewood Suites, 3100 Parkway
Boulevard, Kissimmee FL 34746. Tel:
(407) 396–2229.

Travelodge, PO Box 22205, Lake
Buena Vista FL 32830. Tel: (407)
828–2424.

Travelodge, Maingate, Kissimmee.

Thomas Cook MasterCard
travellers' cheques free you from the
hazards of carrying large amounts of
cash, and in the event of loss or theft
can quickly be refunded (see
**Emergencies and Emergency Phone
Numbers**). Travellers' cheques must be
denominated in US dollars and are
widely accepted in lieu of cash. The

following branch of Thomas Cook can
provide emergency assistance: Thomas
Cook Travel, 1900 Summit Tower
Boulevard, Suite 130, Orlando, FL
32810.

OPENING HOURS

Being geared to the holidaymaker,
many shops, especially in areas like
International Drive and around Church
Street Station, tend to keep very late
hours, so you can buy a pair of jeans
even at 10pm. Elsewhere, usual opening
times are from 9–10am to 6–8pm,
Monday to Saturday. Many shops, and
especially the main shopping malls, also
open on Sundays.

Major theme park opening hours
vary greatly, depending on seasonal
demand, and may change at short
notice. Check carefully during your
stay, or you could be caught out.

Some museums close on Mondays.

PHARMACIES

You can buy simple medicines at any
drug store, though certain drugs
generally available elsewhere require a
prescription in the US.

Sometimes two wheels are better than four

and through mail offices, which usually open from Monday to Friday 8.30/9am to 5pm, and Saturday to noon. US mail boxes are blue in colour.

The US Mail can be notoriously slow. Allow anything from a week to 10 days for air mail letters to reach Europe. Postcards take even longer. It is important to use zip (post) codes and to write clearly, preferably printing the name and address. If you are sending a parcel home, you will need to complete the appropriate customs declaration form.

Post restante (general delivery)
You can arrange for mail to be held for you at any post office. It must be addressed to include the post office's zip code and will be held for you for up to 30 days. Proof of identity is required when you collect.

Telegrams (wires)
Telegrams are still an important service in the USA. Western Union and ITT will take wire messages by phone. Toll-free numbers can be found in telephone directories.

PUBLIC HOLIDAYS
1 January – New Year's Day
15 January – Martin Luther King Day
3rd Monday in February – George Washington's birthday
last Monday in May – Memorial Day
4 July – Independence Day
1st Monday in September – Labor Day
2nd Monday in October – Columbus Day
11 November – Veterans' Day
4th Thursday in November – Thanksgiving Day
25 December – Christmas Day.

POLICE
'Orlando's finest' drive green and white cars and patrol on foot and bicycle. The 'State Troopers' of the Highway Patrol are responsible for major roads and dealing with traffic violations. Many hotels, shopping malls and other businesses employ armed private security guards.

In an emergency, dial 911 and ask for the police. For less urgent matters, police station addresses and phone numbers are listed in telephone directories.

POST (MAIL) OFFICES
Stamps are sold through a wide range of retail outlets, including supermarkets,

PUBLIC TRANSPORT

Orlando is a city geared very much to the automobile, though Lynx Tri-County Transit (tel: (407) 841–8241) operates buses throughout the area and have introduced a new route providing very frequent services along International Drive.

RELIGIOUS WORSHIP

Many Americans are very religious and, given the wide diversity of their ethnic backgrounds, there is a profusion of places of worship serving most religions and denominations, as well as an abundance of religious programmes to be found on TV.

Some problems have been experienced through visitors being hassled by representatives of some of the more unconventional sects. Unless you are genuinely interested it is best to give a firm but polite 'NO'. Avoid being drawn into lengthy discussions.

Roadside wit – but driving here is quite tame by European standards

SENIOR CITIZENS

Whilst Orlando is a paradise for young holidaymakers, its initial attraction was to the elderly – both as a relaxing holiday destination and as a place to retire. Discounts and benefits (often quite generous) are frequently offered to senior citizens (55 and over) for travel, accommodation, entrance fees to attractions and the like. If no such offers are listed, it is worth asking in any case. Also ask your travel agent about special concessions.

STUDENT AND YOUTH TRAVEL
Specialist reduced-rate travel and student
exchange programmes are offered by
tour operators. Likewise, museums,
galleries and attractions offer student
discounts. There is just one youth hostel
in Orlando (see page 171).

TELEPHONES
These days, phoning home could not be
simpler. British Telecom now offer a
charge card which enables you to direct
dial from almost anywhere in the world
by keying in your pin number, the
charges being added to your usual
quarterly telephone bill. Phone
companies in other countries have
similar schemes. Several different,
competing phone companies operate in
Florida, patching into the international
network. If you call abroad 'collect'
(transfer charge) via the operator, you

will be asked which company you wish
to use, to which it is best to respond:
'The one offering the lowest charge for
this call please'.

Public phones take 5c, 10c and 25c
coins and can be found in hotel lobbies,
waiting rooms, big stores, train and bus
stations, airports, as well as on the
street. Most of Orlando comes within
the 407 area code – calls outside this
area cost more. For local calls, there is
no need to add the area code when
dialling. Zone calls are those numbers
within the same area code that are
classified as non-local, ie a good
distance away. These are quite
expensive and may require you to dial
1 before the number.

Long-distance calls within the US
are expensive but off-peak rates operate
from 6–11pm and cheap rates from
11pm–8am. Dial 1 + area code + phone
number. For collect (reverse charge)
calls, where the person at the other end
will pay for the connection.

For international direct dial calls,
dial 011 + country code + area code +
number. Country codes from US to
Britain: 44; Ireland 353; Australia 61;
New Zealand 64; Canada 1.

For the international operator, dial
(1–800) 874–4000.

Lots of tourist attractions,
commercial companies and public
offices offer a toll-free (freephone)
number prefixed by 800 or 1–800,
followed by the number or letter
sequence (eg 1–800 WDISNEY). Such
numbers only operate within the US.

Many exchanges are now wholly
automated. Trying to get hold of a real-
life operator can be frustrating as you
will be answered by a disembodied
voice which will offer some nugget of
often unwanted information followed by

some other digits to dial for further help, often from yet another computer-synthesised voice.

TIME
Orlando is on Eastern Standard Time (five hours behind Britain; six hours behind Western Europe; 15 hours behind Australia; 17 hours behind New Zealand). US Daylight Saving Time is operated, with clocks moving forward an hour from the first Sunday in April to the last Sunday in October.

Don't be caught out by the US convention of month/day/year dates, ie 6–5–95 is 5 June 1995, not 6 May 1995!

TIPPING
This is part of the American way of life. Taxi drivers and hairdressers expect 15 per cent, waiting staff between 15 and 20 per cent. Bellhops, doormen and airport porters will also expect a tip (minimum 50c per bag). When paying by credit card, add the tip to the total before signing the slip.

TOILETS
Whether known as 'the bathroom', 'the rest room' or, colloquially, 'the john', these are usually of a very high standard and clean. Public toilets are unknown, except within airports and bus and train stations. Use those at bars, restaurants and filling stations.

TOURIST OFFICES
The Orlando Visitors Information Center, Mercado Mediterranean Shopping Village, 8445 International Drive (tel: (407) 363–5876) opens year round from 8am–8pm and is the fount of all knowledge, offering up-to-date information and advice, brochures and a discount ticket and booking service.

There is another well-stocked office at Kissimmee, representing the Kissimmee–St Cloud Convention and Visitor's Bureau; 1925 West Irlo Bronson Memorial Highway (US 192), open: daily 8am–6pm; tel: (1–800) 333–KISS.

Unconventionally dressed bellhop